A Blossom from a Barnyard

A Blossom from a Barnyard

▼

Judith Lynn Sanson

Writers Club Press
San Jose New York Lincoln Shanghai

A Blossom from a Barnyard
All Rights Reserved © 2001 by Judith Lynn Sanson

No part of this book may be reproduced or transmitted in any form or by any means, graphic, electronic, or mechanical, including photocopying, recording, taping, or by any information storage retrieval system, without the permission in writing from the publisher.

Writers Club Press
an imprint of iUniverse.com, Inc.

For information address:
iUniverse.com, Inc.
5220 S 16th, Ste. 200
Lincoln, NE 68512
www.iuniverse.com

ISBN: 0-595-16760-8

Printed in the United States of America

I dedicate this book to my family Tom, Tommy, and Phillip. To my friends Mary, Meg, Janis & her daughter. To my sisters and to my Father who showed me nothing is impossible. And all respect to all the small farmers of America.

Contents

Chapter 1. Going to the Farm 1
Chapter 2. Our Forty-Acre Farm. 8
Chapter 3. Getting Started 17
Chapter 4. With Growth Comes Sacrifice 25
Chapter 5. A Long Summer 31
Chapter 6. Reading, Writing and Friends 42
Chapter 7. Going to an Auction 52
Chapter 8. The Blossom Farm-Early Summer of 1969 64
Chapter 9. Our Second Autumn- Of 1969 74
Chapter 10. Grandma and Grandpa's House 86
Bibliography. 93
Index 95

Chapter 1

▼

Going to the Farm

The wind whipped through my hair, the pounding hooves beneath my feet. We flew like a Pegasus. The long flaxen mane had slapped and stung my face. I hung tight on this beautiful steed, like a toy cowboy on a toy horse." Hi-ho Flicka" I hollered out to the world.

The steed took me quickly through plush rolling hills we stopped. He reared and I leaned forward into his neck.

"Judy, stop leaning on me." Charmon said as she pushed against me.

"Charmey, don't push me. Oh, where am I anyway?" I whined.

"Judy, don't you remember. We're going to our new farm" Charmon answered.

"Oh, I forgot where I was. I had such a neat dream, I yawned and stretched.

"Well, what did you dream about?" Charmon whispered.

"I was riding the most beautiful horse through the rolling hills. I wish you never woke me up!" I said as I rubbed my tired eyes.

"Oh, I hope we get a pony," Charmon held her hands together and giggled.

"You two, please be quiet back there!" requested Dad.

"We will make a stop as soon as possible," He reassured us looking in the rearview mirror. We were excited and bored at the same time. Dad leaned over and whispered something to Ma. She glanced back, and shook her head up and down then looked at Dad. Soon, the big red station wagon with our big trailer loaded down with our furniture began to slow down. We all got excited; it finally was time to fuel up. We sounded like a school bus full of children.

"Yeah, it's our favorite gas station," Bud yelled.

The gas station had a snake and lizard painted on the front of the building. A big sign read "Gas, Groceries, and Reptiles."

"Now, kids, we're not stopping long. Just long enough to fuel up, get some groceries, use the restrooms, and stretch our legs," said Dad. "Stay close together and don't wander off too far. We're getting back on the road soon. Ellen, could you get us some sandwich makings and something to drink?"

"Okay, my Darling," Mom replied cheerfully, reaching over giving Dad a kiss. Dad got out to fuel up the car, checked the oil, and put air in the tires. We got out and ran into the building. The first place everyone had to go was the restroom. We stood in line according to age. Ma was always first and then youngest to the oldest. Bud was 7 yrs. I was 9 yrs Charmon was 10yrs. Ann was 12 yrs. and Nyla was 13 yrs old.

Afterward we had the freedom to explore and check the place out. The first room we walked into was a small room full of a variety of aquariums. It had a reptile smell, like going to the zoo. On the left side of this room was a doorway that said "Grocery's" above it and souvenirs were everywhere. No matter where you walked aquariums full of every type reptiles, snakes, lizards and fish lined the walls on the shelves.

The neatest thing was in the middle of the room. On a huge wooden tree stump, was a large, metal washbasin. You could hear splashing and growling in it. It was mounted high enough so that little children could not put their hands in it. A sign hung above the basin. In bold print it stated "DO NOT PUT YOUR HANDS IN THE BASIN". We all stood around the basin on our tiptoes trying to look in.

"Pick me up, I want to see them!" whined Bud. Nyla reached around Bud's waist and picked him up. He grunted as she lifted him, to the large metal basin full of growling reptiles.

"Now, Bud don't put your fingers in there or they will bite them off," giggled Nyla. We all surrounded the tub with our eyes and mouths wide open.

"Wow, aren't they cute?" I asked as I struggled to look into the basin, hanging on the edge of it with my fingertips

"Well, I think they're ugly," Ann said wrinkling her nose.

"I want one for a pet!" I begged and jumped up and down a little, hanging onto the basin.

"Judy, you know Daddy won't let you have a baby alligator," Nyla smiled.

"Yeah, you'd probably walk around without fingers on your hands," Charmon giggled.

Dad and Mom were at the cash register and paid for the gas and groceries. "I'll wait for you and the kids in the car," said Mom as she took the groceries and walked out to the car. Soon, Dad smiled and slowly walked over to see what we were giggling about.

"So what are you kids looking at?" He looked down at the basin and smiled at us.

"Now that's a lot of alligators and, no, you can't have one!" He laughed. "Did all you kids go to the bathroom?" He asked as he crossed him arms and thumped his foot.

"Yes, we did!" Nyla answered quickly.

"Alright, let's get in the car, we have a long way to go," he requested. We all loaded in the order that we first got in at the beginning of the trip. Ann and Nyla sat by the windows and Charmon and I sat between them. Bud sat between Mom and Dad. Everything was ready to go and soon we were back on the road and on our way. This time the trip was different from the last few moving trips. I sat there thinking about Muckwonago, remembering neat things about the town. We were no longer returning back to this town we left for good this time. Mom had made some bologna sandwiches and handed them out to us and gave us something to drink.

"Charmon, I can't wait until we get to our farm, but I'm still going to miss our friend Jeanie," I said and took another bite of bologna sandwich.

"Yeah, me too but I hope we get a pony." Said Charmon as she took a bite and smiled.

Then we sat there with full stomachs thinking quietly about the friends and the times we had left behind. I smiled and thought about the time. I rode old Betsy uptown, an old hand-me down bicycle with balloon tires. She was painted a powder blue. Every time I got my nickel or dime allowance, I use to ride old Betsy uptown to the dime store. I would buy a toy for a nickel and two pieces of Bazooka bubblegum for a penny.

Many businesses circled an island in the middle of the town. That is where they put a display of baby Jesus, at Christmas time. When you entered the town was a Mobile gas station on the right. Behind it was a large gray building, it was the towns, riding stable. A small street dipped down and around the old gray building that needed a paint job. At the bottom of the hill was the entrance: old gray doors hung on the rusty old hinges. The pasture was across from this building entrance. The little street ran between the pasture and the building. There were plenty of horses in this pasture. Soon there was a nudge on my arm.

"Hey, Judy! We're getting closer to our farm," whispered Charmon. We both noticed Dad's tired blood shot eyes, gazing at us in the rearview mirror and that meant quiet.

"Shush!" I whispered.

I couldn't help but think about the time when Charmon and I went to the end of the pasture and walked up to this beautiful white horse. He was very friendly and met us part way walked up to both of us. I found an old twine string on the ground; we both slowly put the twine around his neck.

"I'm riding first because I found the twine on the ground," I insisted.

"Okay, have it your way," Charmon answered stubbornly.

Just as I was attempting to mount, a tall man in a red shirt had come out of the barn and started to call for his horse. The white horse, we had caught perked up his ears, pulled away from us and galloped with his tail up in the air toward the man.

"Charmon, I forgot the twine on his neck. Do you think he saw us?" I covered my mouth a second and started to bust out laughing.

"I don't know but I'm not going to find out!" she screamed. We both giggled and ran through the barbwire fence like two scared jackrabbits. The car then slowed down and made another rest stop, we all climbed out of the car. I smiled.

"Charmon I'm thinking about Muckwonago and the times we had there," I said and she smiled.

"Girls, hurry up! We'll be there, in about an hour and a half," Dad and Mom hurried us. We all got back into the car to finish our journey. As I sat quiet and felt tired, and still very bored. I heard a car screech its tires. I remembered the time when I crossed the street and had gotten hit by a car. Charmon ran across the street before I did. I got caught behind on the other side of the street. That day was as clear to me as if it were yesterday. And yet it happened to me when I was in 1st grade I was 6 years old.

"Hurry, Judy we're going to be late for school," Charmon waved me over. I was so scared I felt so alone, I had to get across, and I couldn't wait any longer.

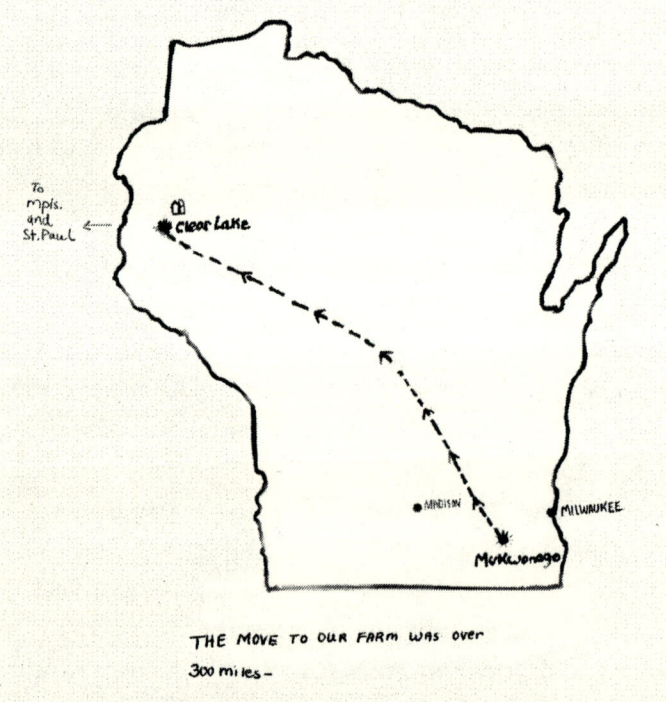

THE MOVE TO OUR FARM WAS over 300 miles—

As I ran to the middle of the street, I didn't see the car. I heard a car screech its tires. I felt a thump on my right hip. I flipped around landing on my side. Immediately I jumped up and started to run.

"Hey, little girl are you okay?" the couple in the car inquired. I heard them and looked for a brief second. I was so scared I just wanted to run. I was so scared I didn't feel any pain. I hurried and caught up to Charmon. Her eyes and mouth were wide open; she looked frantic.

"Judy, are you okay? You did a whole back flip!" Charmon looked shaken.

"Did I? I feel fine. I'm just a little stiff," I replied, "Let's go!" I felt so scared as a deer would. I just wanted to run and not look back. We were both scared and started to run. When we heard someone holler behind us.

"Hey, little girl are you okay?" We turned and looked. There were two men running toward us, like Batman and Robin one was taller than the other. We looked back at them. We were scared and had to get to school. We started running as fast as we could. We made it to school that day okay. The school called my mom that evening. She checked me out for any bruises. I guess God was looking out for me; I didn't even get a bruise.

Yes, I remembered that day very clearly. Thinking goodbye and farewell, to the town with it's memories. Now it's a new town and a new home. I stared at the back of the seat and drifted off to sleep, for another nap.

"Judy, wake up were almost in the driveway," Nyla nudged as hard as she could. The car was starting to slow down and the left blinker started to blink like a thumping drum beat. We all sat high in our seats, looking out the windows. The excitement was tingling like a bubble ready to burst.

Chapter 2

Our Forty-Acre Farm

The car slowly drove in the short driveway on the left of the driveway entrance was a plush little woods. The right side of the driveway, were a row of huge maple trees that provided shade for the driveway. The first building we approached was a small white cottage, that Dad called the summer kitchen. On the right side of the cottage was a narrow gray outhouse. The car had finally come to a stop in front of our new little plum colored house. The cottage was kiddy-corner from the house. A garage stood behind the cottage and was directly facing toward the house. The car doors flew open; we all jumped out at the same time to stretch and breathe the fresh, sweet air.

We looked around and saw a towering shadow. It crossed the driveway touching the roof of the house. The tall giant spun its top as if was in a hurry. The windmill sang its squeaky song as it spun around. As if it was welcoming us to our new home. We all gazed at it a little while, watching it with our hands shadowing our eyes. On the side the windmill stood a little white building.

"That's our milk house," Dad said, stood, pointing, and proudly smiling.

Before he could say more, we scattered like mice. We all ran toward the big red barn, which was across from the little white milk house. We ran and jumped because we were so happy.

"Thank you God for our farm!" Charmon and I grabbed each other's hands and jumped around in a circle. We ran to the barn and swung the door open. Kerblam it hit against the wall of the barn and shook the windows. We couldn't believe our eyes when we looked inside; it was dusty, dirty and full of cobwebs. The gutters were full of old hay the old wooden stanchions were falling apart. The stanchions were about four foot tall. They looked like giant clamps. They held the cow in place so the farmer could milk them and release when he was done.

"Boy, this looks nothing like Uncle Johnny's grade "A" dairy barn," I replied feeling very disappointed.

"You know, Dad said he was going to fix up the barn and get a herd of milking cows like Uncle Johnny," Charmon said as she reached over to turn on the porcelain light switch covered with about an inch of heavy dust. The walls were made of old logs with old cement and manure in between them for insulation.

"Well, at least the lights work and Dad won't have to fix them," I laughed.

"Let's go see what's behind the barnyard door!" said Charmon she started to turn to race.

"Okay, Charmon, I'll beat you to the door!" We raced inside the dusty old barn. We opened the back door and the door slammed against the outside wall and shook the windows. We went back to the front entrance and jumped out the back. We looked around and saw a cement walk. We looked around and saw a cement walk surrounded by a dirt barnyard. On the left side stood a big cement silo.

A barbwire gate was hooked up to a post by the silo. The gate was connected to a four-strand barbwire fence that lead out to a big maple tree. A stock tank for watering the animals sat a few feet from the barbwire fence. The fence lined up to a huge maple tree and old cow paths followed the one side of the fence. The fence turned left and there on its side laid a giant oak tree that was still alive. It looked like a tornado had pushed it over. The fragrance of lilac was in the air. The warm wind was softly blowing.

The tree was so neat; it looked better than monkey bars in a playground. We couldn't help ourselves it was as if that big tree was calling to us and waving its leaves. "Come play with me," the tree would beg to us, the leaves were blowing in the wind.

"Charmon, I'll race you to that cool looking tree!" I yelled and started running. We ran as fast as our legs could carry us. The soft dust on the cow path under our feet puffed in the air. We turned about the big maple tree. A few feet away was the gentle giant. It waved its green leaves to us as if it was talking to us. We got right up to it and there was someone already playing on it.

"Hey, Bud how did you get here so fast?" Charmon puffed.

"Gosh, I was hoping it was a monkey," I gasped to catch my breath.

"Ha ha, I beat you guys!" Bud laughed as he hung upside down like a monkey.

We started to climb on the huge trunk branches that were everywhere. I felt like a squirrel, as I ran up the trunk. Climbing felt easy the trunk felt rough beneath my feet.

"Hey, Charmon isn't this great? I'm hungry for some nuts, ya got any?" I felt gitty.

"No, but I feel hungry for some bananas. You have any?" said Charmon, hanging upside
down on a large branch and swinging back and forth.

"Yes, I have no bananas. I have no bananas today!" I sang while hanging on a branch.

"Hey, look at me I'm on the tallest branch!" Bud sat up as high as he could.

"Hey, Charmon, Judy, Bud, time for supper!" Dad hollered loud and his voice echoed.

"Were coming," we hollered back. Slowly, we got down and started to run back to the house when we noticed a couple more cars parked there. I bet Grandma and Grandpa Chovan, Uncle Danny and Aunt Hazel. Aunt Kitty, Uncle Calvin and Uncle Leo with our dog, Blacky, are here. Blacky was brought up from our last trip and brought over to Grandma and Grandpa's house until we brought the last load up. We had potluck for dinner then. Everyone helped us unload and put things away. It gave us more time to play and explore. Soon everyone left and it was late time to go to bed. We all gave Mom and Dad a kiss and thanked them for getting this nice farm.

"Daddy, can we get a pony?" I begged when I gave Dad his kiss goodnight.

"It's too soon to say, but we'll see," Dad quietly as he yawned and smiled. I woke up the next morning to a sound of a bumblebee; our bunk beds were sitting by the window. But it wasn't a bumblebee instead it was a ruby-throated hummingbird. Somehow the little fellow got through a small hole in the screen and within a few minutes he had found his way out.

"Charmon, wakeup and smell that Folgers's coffee," I said as I took a big whiff.

"Smell that bacon, eggs, and I bet coffeecake," Charmon said as she inhaled the aroma.

"Hey girls, time to get up for breakfast!" Ma hollered.

"We'll be right down, Mom!" Charmon answered.

We hurried up, jumped out of bed, and stumbled to the bathroom. Everyone beat us to the breakfast table. Dad sat at the head of the table and Ma was serving breakfast. We had more than enough to eat. The coffeecake had brown sugar and melted butter smothering it. The essence was sweet, buttery, and had a hint of cinnamon. The bacon was on a platter, greasy and crispy, just the way Dad loved it. The eggs were scrambled, seasoned, and fried in bacon grease. The sweet cold orange juice added the right touch to a perfect breakfast, the first on our new farm.

"Kids, stay out of trouble today. I need to rest. Nyla and Ann, you know what you're suppose to do," Dad said while he took another cup of coffee and slowly drank it.

"May we be excused from the table, Dad?" Nyla asked politely.

"You may all be excused from the table," replied Dad.

"I'll race all of you guys to the barn and the last one is a rotten egg!" Nyla challenged. We tore away from the kitchen table as fast as we could go. The door slammed behind each of us, one at a time. Ann started to help Mom pick up the dishes and clear the table.

"I'll join you guys in a little bit. I'm helping Mom," Ann replied as she picked up plates.

"Listen to that. It's quiet, and smell that fresh cut hay and lilacs. Close your eyes and feel that warm breeze." said as Nyla stood there and took a big deep breath and enjoyed the essence.

We heard the screen door open and there stood Dad. He was of medium stocky build and stood about 5 foot 8 inches tall. His dark colored hair was thin on top and his side burns were trimmed. He looked exhausted; his hazel eyes were and had bags under them. We started to run toward the barn but instead, we waited for Dad to give us instructions.

"I want you girls to run over to the neighbor and buy a gallon of milk, here's fifty-cents!"

"His name is Alvin Hurtle. He's a nice person so don't be afraid. You all can go over," Dad said and yawned. He closed the door and went back into the house. We all started to run down the short driveway to cross the wide dirt road. It was about 9:00 am. and you could hear the hum in Alvin's milk house start up. Alvin stood there about six foot tall with a strong build.

His hands were strong, callused and rough looking. His eyes were a light blue and his face was gentle and kind. He wore a brimmed farmer's hat that covered his pale blonde hair. He had started to take his two silver Surge milk buckets into the barn.

"Well, now what do we have here?" He stood there, holding a bucket, with a pleasant smile on his face.

"Our Dad sent us over to meet you and buy a gallon of milk. Here's fifty cents," We said Nyla then handed him the money. He took it and slid it into his pocket. He sat the bucket down so he could reach into the big silver bulk tank. He took our gallon glass Miracle Whip jar and gracefully dipped it into the fresh creamy milk, thick with butterfat.

"Yummy, that smells good," Bud took a big whiff as Mr. Hurtle pulled it out of the bulk tank.

"It's really nice to meet you kids, but I must go milk the girls, and clean the barn." He then grabbed his bucket and walked into his barn to start his chores.

We ran out of the milk house and looked both ways as we crossed the dirt road. Nyla carried the warm milk carefully so not to drop it. We all walked back together.

"He seemed like a nice man," Charmon said as she walked with a hop in her step.

"Yep, he seems pretty nice," Nyla cautiously replied.

"I liked his farm. He had some real big Holstein cows. They are so pretty," I felt playful I wanted to jump. I wanted to fly. I was tingling with joy of our own farm.

"I liked his John Deere "B" tractor. Its just like Grandpa's tractor!" Bud said as he ran to the yard and rolled on his back under the big shade tree by the house.

Charmon and I sat in the cool, soft grass under a big Maple tree, while Nyla took the milk into the house.

"Charmon, what should we do today? Explore?" I asked while sitting in the soft grass under a big tree.

"Let's see what Nyla wants to do first," Charmon stretched. We did some exploring that day went hiking, checked out the buildings and more adventures await us tomorrow.

That night I started to write in my diary, a going away gift from Jeanie. I wondered that night who my friends were going to be and what things were going to be like. I thought about those who were left behind.

Dear Diary   May 30, 1968

Its been quite an experience. Moving was hard work. I will no longer be a city slicker but a country girl. Maybe we will get that pony now since we got the land. I love our new farm and the way the air smells. I will miss Jeanie and sometimes I feel lonely not having her for a neighbor. I love our windmill and how it blows in the wind. I love our new little barn and I bet it holds about eleven cows. It's so exciting and change can be good. Just think, I'm nine years old and we're hopefully going to be dairy farmers some day soon.

"Judy, are you done yet? I'm tired and ready to get some sleep!" Charmon said as she tucked under the covers.

"And turn off the light!" Charmon inquired. I got up and pulled the string attached to the light. Another day was done. Tomorrow will be another exciting day.

Chapter 3

▼

Getting Started

"Wow, just look at the size of these raspberries! They're about the size of strawberries!" I said as I picked one. It filled the palm of my small hand.

"They're so sweet and juicy. Hey Judy, look at my hands! They're pink" Charmon smiled.

"Charmon, look at this little tree frog. He landed on my hand while I was picking raspberries." I studied him carefully, observing his fine little structure. "Look isn't he cute, a dark lime green with a yellow belly, he's so smooth," I added.

"Look, there a couple more, it looks like about five of them," Charmon counted.

"Hey, you two get out of those raspberries. Ma will kill you if she found out that you guys were in them!" Ann yelled as she ran out of the house. She stood about five foot tall with slender features. Ma's little blonde haired beauty queen, with a disposition of a cat.

"Ann, we were not eating raspberries, we were catching little tree frogs." Charmon commented as she shrugged her shoulders as she continued to eat the raspberries quickly. Pink around her mouth and a smirk on her face.

"Sure you are. Let me see what you were really up to!" Ann said she grabbed our hands to see pink raspberry stains on our palms and fingers. We tried to pull our hands away from her in a hurry to hide the evidence.

"Yum, these are very good," Ann, said as she tried a small handful they were spilling to the ground. She kept grabbing them and stuffing them into her mouth, smiling. "I won't tell if you don't, what's this about tree frogs?" Ann, questioned while Charmon grabbed one and threw it on Ann's neck, it clung on.

"Hey, get that thing off my neck!" Ann started dancing with a tree frog clinging to the nap of her neck. "Hey, who put that frog on my neck!" Ann kept bouncing around like a kangaroo.

"She hops like a kangaroo!" I shouted as we burst out laughing so hard. Almost rolling to the ground.

"Ann, Judy did it!" Charmon laughed holding her stomach.

"Oh, no it was Charmon! Ann, you sure looked funny!" I held my stomach.

"It really doesn't matter who done it, but those little frogs sure stick to you," Ann started to laugh, thinking how funny she looked. She then picked one up and started to look at it. The little frog sat balanced on her finger breathing quickly, looking to jump off. He jumped off onto a raspberry leaf it swayed.

Ann said "Oh they're so cute. But before I forget, I'm supposed to tell you guys to get ready to go Uncle Johnny's at two o'clock. That's in fifteen minutes. We're going to get a couple of calves from him,"

"Okay, we'll hurry!" I answered and hurried to beat Charmon to the bathroom to wash up. That afternoon, we all got into our yellow stub nose Dodge pickup truck and drove over to Uncle Johnny and Aunt Gladys's farm. We all fit into the cab: Dad drove and Nyla, Ann, and Ma sat by the door, and Charmon, Bud and I sat on their laps. It was like a three-ring circus when all those clowns climbed out of a little tiny car. But this was the Ford family, all seven of us in a small cab of a truck.

Uncle Johnny and Aunt Gladys lived outside of Glenwood City, Wisconsin. It was 25 miles south from Clear Lake, where we lived. We arrived there about 2:40 that afternoon, in time. So Dad could help Uncle Johnny with the cow milking. Uncle Johnny always appreciated extra help and taught Dad about milking cows. Uncle Johnny and Aunt Gladys were Moms aunt and uncle.

Aunt Gladys was a very good cook and was always very kind and hospitable. She could put on a spread that could feed an army. Her brother, Harold, was their hired hand. He would help Uncle Johnny do field work. Milk the cows and other chores. He was always grumpy and had no patience for children.

They also had a large German shepherd named King. He was big brown with black on his back legs and face. Uncle Johnny would swear that he was the best cow dog he had ever seen because he was smart. Uncle Johnny would say, "King, go bring the cows in!" King would get up from his nap, perk his ears up from under the kitchen table and run out the screen door. In minutes, King would run find the herd and bring them in. It didn't matter how steep the hill or how rocky the terrain King got his cows. Later that day, Uncle Johnny called to King, and pointed to a cow on the hill.

"I want that cow up there, King, go get her!" King ran up the hill and the cow tried to bunt him. He somehow grabbed her by her head and totally flipped that cow, sending her rolling down the hill. The cow stood up swinging her head like she was dizzy and she walked around like she was drunk. Then she saw King and ran toward the barn. Charmon and I just couldn't believe our eyes. It was so impressive that we laughed. The cows were now in the barn eating their feed. We all went up to the house to have supper.

"Now where have you kids been?" "I haven't seen you two since you've gotten here!" Aunt Gladys said as she looked at us with her thick wire rimmed glasses and her dark salt and pepper curly hair. She pointed and shook a spoon at us with her hand on her hip. "My have you two grown, you two could pass as twins!" Aunt Gladys shook and. laughed

"Charmey. Judy. My how you both have gotten taller!" She said as she started to scoop the beans.

"Look, at that blonde hair, and your both about the same height and on the scrawny side,"

"We can't help it if we look alike. Everyone calls us twins, "Charmon replied and grinned.

"Ann, you're looking prettier every day," said Aunt Gladys and Ann's face turned a little red.

"Nyla, you're looking more like your Dad. Your hair is so dark brown," replied Aunt Gladys Nyla smiled. Then continued to eat her supper.

"Nyla sounds more like a sergeant every day and always a grouch!" Charmon added.

"Boy, does Nyla have the muscles her Dads right hand man," Uncle Johnny grinned.

"Show us your muscles, Nyla," Aunt Gladys laughed. Nyla then raised her right arm, folded her arm over, and extended her biceps. Bud grabbed her arm trying to make it collapse.

"Wow, I sure wouldn't want to get in a scrap with her," Uncle Harold laughed.

"We're full, May Charmon and I be excused from the supper table, Dad?" I asked.

"Yes, you may," Dad said as he drank some coffee and continued to finish eating his roll. Then we got up, pushed our chairs in and walked out the screen door. It slammed behind us. King followed us out practically knocking us over.

"Charmon and I are going to see the rabbits!" I hollered into the house.

"Okay, but stay out of the chicken coop, and don't bother those chickens," Aunt Gladys hollered.

"We will, Aunt Gladys," we both answered.

"Hey Charmon, here's King. Let's have him bring us a cow like Uncle Johnny,"

Getting Started 21

"Yeah, let's have King get that cow over there on the hill," we pointed to a big Holstein cow, on the hill. King got excited and started barking. He then charged up the steep hill, by the barnyard. He nipped at her heels barked at her, and she let out a loud "moo!" She came running down the hill almost tumbling. Soon the screen door slammed and it was Uncle Harold. He stood there observing King; he took his hat off and scratched his head.

"King, get over here!" Uncle Harold grumbled. King was soon at his feet, panting, wagging his tail waiting for the next order, and willing to respond.

"Hey, who told King to do that?" He looked at both of us, as we started to scuff the ground and look at our feet.

We both looked at Uncle Harold and shrugged our shoulders. "I don't know," Charmon answered in a little voice. We looked at each other and scuffed our feet.

Uncle Harold shook his head as he walked up to the old red barn on the hill. He went to set up the barn for milking. He started the vacuum pump and put the milkers on the walkway. Soon Uncle Johnny and Dad came out of the screen door, talking as they went up the barn to start the milking. The cows were turned out of the barn as they were milked.

"Charmon, let's go up that big hill and roll down it," I exclaimed as I jumped up and down.

"Okay, I'll race you to the hill. Last one is a rotten egg!" Charmon yelled as she turned and started to run. To get to the hill we had to go through an obstacle coarse; first, we had to clear a big flock of chickens, without tripping. Then we had to get over an old pile of planks and avoid some nails. Next we had to squeeze through three strands of rusty old barbwire fence without tearing clothes.

Then we had to jump around large rocks protruding everywhere throughout the pasture without breaking our necks. When we got to the hill, we had to struggle up it. We finally crawled and gasped to get to the top. We looked down the hill and realized that there were more rocks than we had thought there had been.

"Charmon, first one to the bottom of the hill is the winner!" I yelled and puffed for a breath.

We both laid down resting before we started to roll down the big rocky grass covered hill. Some areas looked smooth, but as we rolled we had to watch where we were going or. We'd hit a rock. We finally struggled down the steep hill around the rocks. We stumbled up on our feet and almost tripped over each other because everything was spinning.

"Charmon, are you dizzy like I 'am? I feel like I'm going to get sick! I think I had enough of that hill," I held my stomach.

"Yep, I feel dizzy too; I'll race you to the barn!" Charmon challenged as she turned to run to the barn. She clumsily started to run, as fast as she could getting a head start.

"Hey, wait a minute! Watch out for that flock geese!" I hollered to her, laughing and started to run to catch up. She started to run through the geese and they nipped at her and chased her. She hurried out of the flock and waited for me to catch up to her.

"Let's go to the barn and see what calves Dad's going to buy!" I grabbed her by the arm and we started to walk and talk about what calves we're going to get. We went through a gate and walked around through the milk house door. They were finishing the milking and on their last cow.

"Baah!" The calves were all bellowing and moaning for their supper. They were so loud the sound echoed through the barn. Uncle Johnny, Uncle Harold and Dad brought these hungry calves each a half of bucket of milk. The calves started sucking on the rubber nipple on the metal bucket. They were bunting the bucket as hard as they could, causing the bucket to drop out of our Dads hands. Thick saliva, white from the milk, drooled, from their mouths. They kept trying to suck on everything they could get a hold of. We walked up to them and they started to suck on our fingers and our clothes, while bunting.

"I like this one Charmon. I hope we get this one," I patted the calf's head because she had soft fur.

"I hope we get this one. She is so cute," Charmon patted the one she liked.

"I don't think Dad wants this one because she looks like a bull," I smiled and pointed at the one in the corner.

"I wonder how many of these Holstein calves Dad wants?" I questioned while quietly started to count.

"There're six big calves here and two of them are bulls," Charmon observed.

"Do you see the heifers we are getting?" Nyla walked over and pointed to four of them. "All of them but those two bulls,"

Dad walked over slowly smiling and admired the nice bunch of calves. Nyla stood by him with her arms folded and he smiled.

"Chores are done let's all go up to the house!" Dad smiled. Nyla took the scraper and cleaned down the walkway for Uncle Johnny.

"That's clean enough, Nyla. Let's go up to the house, where your Aunt's waiting for us," said Uncle Johnny. Harold was out with the tractor and chopper getting fresh cut grass green chop for the cows. It was about 8:30 p.m. and everyone was back into the kitchen. Aunt Gladys did it again; the table was so full of every kind of food, such as deserts, cheeses, and cakes. We ate again until we couldn't eat any more. It was now time to go home we thanked them for a great meal and a good evening. Dad backed the truck to the barn. We loaded our calves and tied them up in the back of the pickup. After getting home late that evening he backed our pickup up to the barn and unloaded our four future dairy cows. We tied them up to different areas in the barn, away from each other. To discourage any calves sucking on each other after a feeding.

"Baah!" The sound echoed loudly through our screen window that next morning.

"Hey, girls it's time to get up I hope you know we got calves to feed now!" Dad stated.

"It's early, Dad. Do we have to?" Nyla whined a little, as she slowly rolled out of bed. He was right; we had to get up at 6:00 a.m. every morning from now on because we didn't inherit a farm and our family wanted one, we were willing to do whatever it takes to get started. That night we fed those calves again about 6:00 p.m.

Dear Diary   June 30,1968

Another, exciting day and soon we will buy more calves. We girls each got a calf given to us. Ann named her heifer Bossy. Nyla named her's Rosebud. Charmon's is Jingle's and mine is named Judy. We also named a couple other calves Impossible and Betsy. Shucks' who would figure that raising a herd of dairy cows could be so much work

Chapter 4

With Growth Comes Sacrifice

In the next few weeks our herd had grown from four to ten. We had purchased three Holstein heifers from our neighbor Alvin Hurtle and three dainty Jersey calves that look like little fawns without the spots from a Jersey farmer. These Jerseys were two heifers and a bull that we named Wrinkles. Caring for calves meant a lot of hard work. We had to get up early and feed them powdered milk. Sometimes they would get sick, and we'd have to give them a scour pill, and extra water so they would not die of dehydration. They would have to nursed back to health. The scour pill saved the calf's life. If we loose a young heifer that meant we'd loose a cow. At 2 months, it was time to wean them so they ate solid calf feed.

When they were all old enough we'd opened the door and put collars on them. We turned them loose out in the pasture. They all got excited and stood in place for a moment and looked around. They would start to run around. They ran so fast they ran everywhere dirt was flying.

"Burp!" Was the sound they would make while kicking their heels and jumping around. They were running into the barbwire fence and bouncing into it like a ball bouncing off a wall. We stood there and laughed. The calves soon settled down to taste grass for the first time.

We had to watch them all day to see that they wouldn't get out that was a full day. The farm was growing slowly but surely. The next day, we had to get up earlier. We checked the calves to see that they hadn't gotten out. We all got into the station wagon and sat there yawning, wondering where we were going.

"Hey Mom, where are we going?" I asked rubbing my eyes.

"We're going grocery shopping up at the Big Bend and to a Hatchery,"

"Good meat prices, right Mom?" Ann added. Ma nodded and smiled.

"But what about the chicks? How many are we going to get?" Nyla asked.

"We're getting 100 White leghorn chicks, so we can eat them and sell the eggs." Dad smiled.

We finally arrived in Minong and we drove right through it. After driving through Hayward we turned right on a dirt road, where a sign read, This way to "Hayward Hatchery." We turned into this nice looking place with gray metal buildings and a little white house. Dad walked up to the house and a tall, older man came out. He directed my dad to back his car up to one of the metal sheds. Soon, he raised the back door of the station wagon. Dad went into the building the old man came out with Dad carrying out two large cardboard boxes. They set the boxes with holes in them on top of each other.

"Chirp, chirp!" The contents of the boxes got louder at each movement. He then shut the back door and the chirping got louder. Dad got back into the car, and we started to head toward home.

"So who's going to butcher these chicks when they get older?" I asked.

"Well, who do you think?" Nyla snapped back.

"Hey, stop picking on her. You're such a grouch!" Ann hollered back.

"Well, you're such a whiny brat, you get everything you want!" Nyla pointed her finger at Ann. Soon; Dad pulled the car to the side of the road and put his arm on the back of the car seat. The chirping had gotten even louder as the car stopped.

"I want you two to quit arguing. You are disturbing the chicks!" Dad turned and hollered.

"Okay Dad, but Nyla started it!" Ann whined. Nyla looked directly at Ann. Her bold stare with those dark hazel eyes. Like it was all Ann's fault. If looks could kill she'd be dead Nyla slowly turned her head. "Enough is enough!" Dad drove on. We stopped in Minong, to get groceries, and fuel up. Finally, we arrived home and Blacky greeted us as we entered the driveway. We backed up to the barn, and opened the barn door, where we unloaded the chicks on to the floor. Dad had a small pen built for them that had a heat lamp hanging over it and two feeders with two plastic water containers. Dad and Nyla took each chick out one by one dipping their beaks into the water. We were introducing them to feed and water. The chicks kept jumping out of the boxes. We reached over and picked one up as Nyla and Dad were counting them as they were taking them out.

"Aren't they cute? So soft, so little, and so light!" I couldn't resist their delicate fragileness. Charmon picked one up and gently hugged it.

"Now carefully set them down. We must keep count," Dad suggested.

"They're so cute," Ann then picked one up to look at it.

The barn door opened and Ma stepped back into the barn and Bud ran back out side to play. For a boy of 7 Years, he was very small with a little round face and big ears. When he smiled his teeth stuck out a little. The youngest could do what he pleased. After Bud ran to play, Mom closed the door behind her so the dog didn't come in. The dog started barking and was running around getting excited.

"Those two pigs are out again! Did someone what to get them in!" Mom urged.

"Oh, I'll get Emily and Arnold in!" Ann volunteered she jumped to her feet.

They were two big pigs, about 150 pounds each and very friendly like big dogs. Ann went out and they followed her back to their pen. Mom stood there by the door, checking to see if Ann managed on her own with the pigs. To see Mom stand there caring about everything around her .She favored wearing a scarf over her dishwater blonde. She had a fine build, fine features, gentle face, and quiet disposition. She was kind and giving and her skills in the kitchen were very versatile. She could cook, rabbit, squirrel, and even pigeon.

"Oh, aren't they darling? I can't wait until they're big enough to eat!" Ma stood over them, tightening the scarf over her short brown hair.

"I think that might be a while yet," Dad smiled and picked one up.

"Well, I'm going up to the house. Is anyone coming up with me?" Ma offered.

"Is it okay if Judy and I go pick some wild raspberries?" Charmon asked.

"Go and bring me some wild raspberries," Ma smiled. " I'll make a pie or something."

"I'll get a couple of ice-cream buckets and we can run out to the woods." Charmon ran up to the house and got the buckets. We hurried up and ran out to the pasture to get to the big woods. We squeezed through a tight barbwire fence and looked for the big raspberry patch. We went to a big oak tree where there was abundance of berries. We were hungry and those berries looked delicious. We started to pick the berries.

"These are so good. Ouch! The bugs are terrible," I slapped my leg.

"It's so hot, it's like sauna out here. It must be 100 degrees!" Charmon said as she wiped her forehead.

"I'm just going to eat them. I hate berry picking. It's too miserable out here". I hit my arm "Ouch!" I'm getting out of here!" I grabbed my bucket and started to run.

"Hey, wait for me!" Charmon started giggling and running. We raced and ducked through the tight barbwire fence.

"I'm hot! I'm going to the creek." The sweat dripped down my face like raindrops. The humidity made it unbearable.

"Last one in is a rotten egg!" I ran as fast as I could, jumping over the rocks.

"Water! It's got water in it! I can't believe it last week it was dry! We must have had enough rain." Charmon yelled. We both ran and jumped into the creek throwing our buckets on the bank. We started splashing water at each other and didn't hear anybody coming.

"Well we really are getting berries, aren't we?" Nyla stood above us looking down She held the .22 rifle on her shoulder and the butt in her right hand.

"Well, what are you going to get this time, Calamity Jane? A rabbit?" I smiled.

"I could bring back anything. A rabbit, a squirrel or a grouse, Judy!" Nyla smiled.

"So if you don't get anything, we'll eat crow or pigeon, right!" Charmon smiled.

"Don't laugh. We could still eat it. Mom will cook it up!" Nyla turned and walked to the woods. We continued to swim and splash in the creek.

"Bang, bang!" The gun went off. "Oh shoot!" Nyla's voice echoed from the woods.

"It sounds like she missed," Charmon laughed.

"Bang!" again echoed from the woods.

"Aw, this water feels so good," Charmon moaned and waved her hands in the creek.

"Hey, are you two going to stay there all day?" Nyla stood there with her hands on her hips. "Did you guys know were going to Grandmas and Grandpas for supper?" She raised her right hand to show a large rabbit. "It's a beauty, isn't it?"

"Looks like rabbit stew tomorrow," Charmon smiled. We got out of the water and started to walk on each side of Nyla, trying to stay on the cow path.

"I bet you guys didn't know that we are on food stamps now!" Nyla replied.

"Does that mean we're poor?" I asked, shadowing my forehead against the sun.

"Dad said it would just be for a little while until we get our farm going." Nyla scratched her head, holding the rabbit in the other hand.

"That's why we don't shop every week like we use to!" Charmon tripped.

"Boy, no more store bought bread. That's why Mom bakes all the time!" I exclaimed as I jumped over the small thistles.

"Judy, it tastes good! I'm not complaining," Nyla licked her lips.

"Girls, its time to get ready to go to Grandmas and Grandpas!" Dad hollered. We all started to run up to the house so we could get ready to go and eat supper.

At our grandparents house we had a hot dish supper and all the Aunts and Uncles were there. After visiting for a while, we went home because dad needed his rest. We also had stuff to do the next day, like weed the big garden and tend to the calves, chicks, chickens, and pigs.

Dear Diary: July 20 1968

Things around here are getting ridiculous. So we don't burn electricity during the day. We're supposed to go out all day to play even if we don't feel like it. I'm getting tired of going over to grandma and grandpa's house. The food is good but there is nothing to do. I'm getting sick of not seeing a grocery store. At least my feet don't hurt anymore after running around barefoot all day.

Chapter 5

A Long Summer

I love our farm and I' am very grateful for living on it. I think back about the other day When Dad got us up earlier so we could get our chores done early. Nyla, Charmon, Bud and I went to Uncle Johnny's farm. We arrived there about 9:00 a.m. and bought seven little pigs from Uncle Johnny. We put them in the back of the pickup. On the way back, we stopped in town, where Dad stopped at the hardware store. He then had red-handled pliers in one hand, and a small white box in the other. He got up to the pickup and asked if all of us could climb in the back of the pickup.

"Now, I want you girls to hold these pigs down for me," Dad put a small brass metal ring in the pliers. "Hold those pigs heads tight while I put these in their noses!" He took the pliers and squeezed it tight on the rim of the nose of the pig. "Wee!" squealed the little white pig. The cry echoed through town as he tried to squirm and wiggle away. Cars drove by very slowly, as if they were curious about the loud squealing. Each pig squealed as we inserted rutting rings in each of their little noses so they wouldn't dig. Later that morning, we brought our new little 30-pound pigs home .Dad had enlarged the pigpen to fit seven more pigs.

"I'm going to town to get some parts so you kids can go play. We're having company later." He then got into the truck to get parts for the car and drove off to town. We all stood there with nothing to do. We looked at the ground kicking rocks around.

"Hey, what do you think we could do?" Nyla asked.

"I don't know. What is there to do? I wish we lived in town," Ann whined.

"Hey, we don't live in town anymore, so be quiet!" Nyla pushed Ann and smiled.

"Don't push me, you better be glad I'm in a good mood," Ann smiled.

"They look like two of the three stooges, don't they," I whispered to Bud and Charmon. Nyla and Ann went over, to talk between themselves laughing and snickering.

"I think Nyla acts like Moe," I started laughing, as I observed my sisters.

"I think Ann acts like Curly! Ha ha!" When Charmon laughed out loud, they glanced at us.

"I wonder what they're up to," whispered Bud as he looked at us.

"You guys come with us. We got a plan," Nyla waved to us, while Ann ran to the barn and came back with a bunch of old twine strings Nyla grabbed Bud by the arm and Ann handed some twine to Nyla

"You two stay there," Nyla said as she turned and whispered something to Bud and walked with him. She took him to the woods in front of the house. We watched for a little while and he didn't come out. Ann then signaled to Charmon, who looked at me and shrugged her shoulders. Charmon and I giggled and Nyla walked over to Ann. Ann took Charmon by the arm and Charmon started smiling, and they walked into the woods. Nyla finally walked out of the woods and called to me, waving her arm.

"Juuudy, its your turn. You're under arrest by the U.S. Marshal. You criminal, come with me!" Nyla grabbed me by the right arm, and walked me into the woods.

"What are going to do to me?" I asked.

"Does it matter? You robbed a bank and will pay for that!" Nyla started to tie my hands behind my back. "Now don't move your hands, or I'll tie it tighter," Nyla commanded.

"Okay, Nyla anything you say!" I replied and feeling silly. Nyla took me around the thick brush and Charmon and Bud were already tied. They're arms and legs were tied and they had gags in their mouths. They were tied up to a couple of small trees. And Blacky was licking their faces; they were smiling but couldn't do anything.

"What, is this?" I asked I felt totally surprised. Nyla then took me to a small tree and ordered me to "sit down," I clumsily sat down.

"Now don't move or I'll tie it tighter," Nyla smirked and tied me to the tree and then tied my legs together. And she took out a kerchief, put it in my mouth and tied it in the back of my head. Blacky came over and licked my face and wagged her tail. "Hee-hee" I giggled because it tickled. Nyla just got up and walked toward the house. We sat there and looked at each other, we heard a car pull in the driveway. Charmon and Bud's eyes looked big and they started to wiggle to get free.

We heard the car doors slam, and people talking. We kept trying to wiggle to get loose. Blacky left us to go up to the house and started barking at the visitors. We could smell spaghetti and garlic bread. We wiggled all the more. Then, we heard another car pull in and Blacky didn't bark this time. Charmon started to break free: One of her hands almost free but the twine was still connected. We heard the car door slam, and knew right away that Dad was home. Soon the screen door slammed and the talking got louder.

"Hi Ben. You're looking good. How's it going?" echoed Grandma's voice from the house. The voices and laughter got louder.

"Where are Charmey, Judy and little Bud?" Grandma asked Dad.

"I don't know. I think they're out there playing somewhere," He answered.

"Gosh, Ben. You better call them in. Supper's about ready," Grandma suggested.

"Yeah Ben, or supper will get cold," Aunt Hazel added.

"Nyla, Ann. Do you know where the other kids are?" Dad asked.

"Well, they're kind of tied up right now!" Nyla smiled.

"They're what? Tied up! I don't believe these kids!" Dad raised his voice and shook his head.

"It's okay. They can get loose," Ann answered.

"Nyla, you better go and untie them because supper is ready," Grandma nagged.

Soon the screen-door slammed and we could hear someone walking down the hill. Nyla walked down the path and into the brush and came over and untied Charmon first.

"Charmon, you untie the rest. I'm going up to eat supper," Nyla asked as she hurried.

"Thank you, Nyla. I thought you were going to forget us out here!" Charmon added.

"Hey, I wanted to forget you guys. More spaghetti for me, but Dad wanted you guys to come up for supper!" Nyla looked at us and winked, than she ran up to the house.

"Are they coming? "Ben, you better do something about those kids!" Grandma added.

"I don't know what to do. They seem a little bored lately. But I got a surprise for them tomorrow," Dad smiled.

"What are you going to do? Get them a motor bike?" Uncle Danny laughed.

"Are ya going to get another cow?" Aunt Hazel teased.

"Well, we're coming back tomorrow to find out the surprise," Grandma laughed. We all walked in, just in time for supper.

"What happened? Did yea get all tied up?" Uncle Danny laughed.

"Nyla and Ann got us tied up, and we couldn't get free," Charmon laughed, feeling embarrassed.

"Boy, that's a nice shade of red!" Aunt Hazel laughed loudly. We finished eating helped clean up the mess, there was plenty of food left over then ran outside. Soon a truck and a trailer turned into the driveway. Blacky started barking, and the truck pulled up by the barn. Dad got up to look out the window; he looked rather surprised.

"Well, I'll be they're not supposed to be here until tomorrow morning! Excuse me folk's" Dad got up, from the chair. Grabbed his hat and went out the door. It slammed behind him.

"Well, he seemed in a hurry. I'm getting out there to find out what's in the truck!" Uncle Danny finished his coffee and ran out the door.

"So am I," said Aunt Hazel as she got up from the table. Her full figure caused the table to be bumped every cup standing fell over. "Oop's!" She said as she ran out the door behind the rest of the group.

We ran over by the truck and were very curious to see what was in the trailer. Dad stood there and talked to the older man. A young girl who had gotten out of the passenger door walked over to where we were standing; .She smiled and stood by us swatting at mosquitoes.

"A beautiful day isn't it? Hi, I'm Cindy Swanson, what's your name's?" She smiled. We were so focused on the trailer I could barely hear her. The back gate of the trailer slowly opened and the creature started to stomp causing the trailer to jerk.

"Oh, I'm Judy and this is Charmon. We're the Ford's," I stood there focusing on the trailer.

"Oh, I can't see. The gate's blocking my view I must stand more to the rear," I said as I sneezed.

"I knew it! It's a horse!" Charmon said as she covered her mouth and we both started to jump around. "He's so beautiful. He's a chestnut. My favorite color red!" I giggled out loud.

"Now calm down kids. You'll each get a chance to ride him," Dad assured us.

"His name is Red. He's a Welch show pony and he has won trophies and ribbons," said Cindy smiling. He was the most beautiful pony I ever did see. He was a brilliant reddish brown with a white cream-colored flaxen mane and tail. He was a solid color he didn't have any white markings.

"He shines and he's so soft," I petted his soft smooth coat and he turned and sniffed my hand.

"His nose is as soft as velvet." I gently petted his forehead and played with his nose.

"Oh, it's just a horse. How boring!" Ann turned and walked up to the house.

"What a fuddy-duddy," Nyla shook her head.

"Oh my what a pretty horse. Oh the mosquitoes are so bad out here," Grandma slapped her arm and, "Well, I better go up and help Ellen," as she walked to the house.

"Thanks for dropping off the pony," Dad said and waved to the visitors as they drove off. Dad took the pony and let Nyla hold him by the lead rope.

"This is a gift to you kids from Mom and I. It's a reward for working hard around the place. Maybe you kid's will stop riding the dang heifers" He patted Nyla on the shoulder and gave her a fifty-dollar smile.

"Thank you. Oh, he's so beautiful," Nyla eyes sparkled at him and petted his soft smooth fur.

"I think he's the most beautiful horse I've ever saw," I patted him on the shoulder.

"I wish I could take him to the fair. I think he would be a good show horse," Charmon patted his forehead and felt his dark velvety soft nose.

"Let's see if we can ride him," Uncle Danny said as he came up to Red.

"Well, it's getting late. You guys can return tomorrow and ride him. Let's have dessert," Dad turned and walked up to the house. They all walked up to the house to get some of the apple pie that Mom had prepared. We proudly took Red and led him around the farm to introduce him to his new home. The windmill started to squeak as a wind picked up. Red jumped forward a little the noise was strange to him. He stiffened up and acted nervous. He snorted at the strange smells; he smelled my hand and seemed to calm down a little. "Whoa Red," Nyla said calmly as she patted Red on the neck.

"Dad, it's getting dark out here. Should we put Red in the pasture?" Nyla hollered through the screen door. Red loudly sniffed the door. He jerked back a little snorting loudly.

"Yeah, go put him out to the pasture," answered Dad as he continued talking to the company.

We took him and walked to the pasture and let him out. He slowly walked out and sniffed around. We turned on the barnyard light to see how he liked his new home. He found some tender green grass and started to eat. It was getting dark and the big yard light was turned on. As we walked to the house Blacky greeted us, panting and wagging her tail. The relatives had their desert and were starting to leave as we slowly walked up to the house. They all stepped out to go to Grandpa's Dodge Dart. It was getting late, but the night was clear. The stars were so bright; we could see all of them.

"My, aren't the stars beautiful tonight?" said Grandma looked up at the stars and rubbed her arms.

"We'll be back tomorrow!" Grandpa replied as he got into the car.

"Thanks for the supper, Ellen," said Aunt Hazel as she waved and got into the car.

The car drove off and we went in and had some dessert and went to the bed. We just couldn't sleep that night. We couldn't believe we got a horse. I kept thinking about riding him through the rolling hills. So we could show him off to the neighbors. Charmon, Nyla and I couldn't wait to get out there to ride Red that next day. We got up very early that next morning and caught Red. We tried to ride him around the pasture but had a very difficult time. We discovered something about Red, but were not going to tell Dad about what that was. Dad and Bud had come out an hour later than we did.

"Oh, I see you girls have already caught Red. Did you get a chance to get on him yet?" asked Dad.

"No, we just caught him out in the pasture," Nyla answered as she held his halter.

"Just hold him a little longer. Bud, come here for a minute," said Dad as Bud slowly walked over to Red. "Gosh, he sure is big," said Bud as he patted Red's neck. Dad held the lead and boosted Bud on Red. Red stood there for a minute; he turned and sniffed Bud's leg.

"I can't watch," I whispered to Charmon. His ears went back and he stiffened his neck, and he started to jump up and down.

"Awe!" Bud hollered and Red threw him into the air like a ball.

"Did you see that"? Said Charmon as she rubbed her eyes.

"Daddy caught him in mid-air like a ball" I rubbed my eyes with disbelief. We walked off together laughing and giggling about what we saw. Soon a couple of cars pulled up. It was all the uncles and aunts; this time Uncle Kelvin and Aunt Kitty were here as well. They walked by the pasture and stood by the wire gate where we had Red tied to a post.

"Oh, I see you got a horse. My Uncle had one of these when I was a kid," Uncle Kelvin smiled. He crawled through the fence and went up to Red and patted him on the neck.

"Go ahead get on him," Uncle Danny waved him on.

"You got a saddle or bridle?" asked Uncle Kelvin. He was so tall he leaned over Red.

"No, I'm afraid not. Get on at your own risk," Dad walked away, shaking his head.

Uncle Danny held Red by the halter, so that Uncle Kelvin could get on. Red turned his head and sniffed Uncle Kelvin's leg. His ears went back and his neck stiffened and he started to jump up and down briskly.

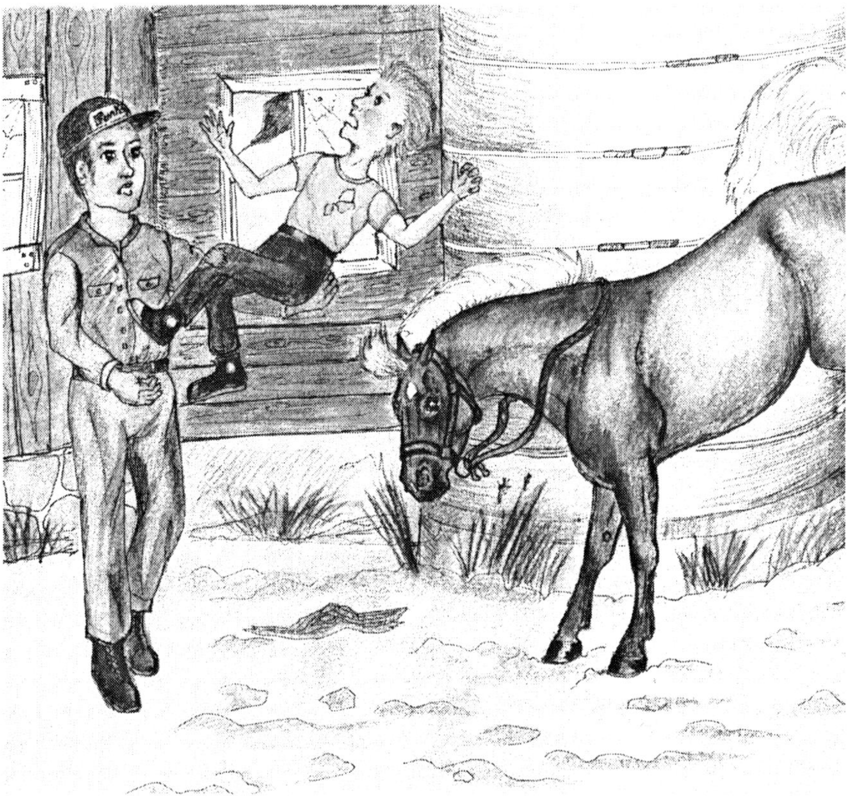

Uncle Danny released the rope and Uncle Kelvin started to sway back and forth. He held on the rope like a broncobuster. Then Red kicked up and Uncle Kelvin went forward. He went flying off his back, then got up, and wiped the dust off his pants. He caught Red by the lead and handed him to Uncle Danny.

"It's your turn to ride this horse," Uncle Kelvin smiled, raising his eyebrows.

Uncle Danny got on Red with the same results. He picked himself up and dusted off his pants. For the full day, everybody who had wanted to brave Red did. This day went very fast, and soon everyone went home. No one had gotten hurt, but they had bruised egos.

Dear Diary: August 10, 1968

I guess God answered our prayers again. We are so happy. We got our first pony. He's a chestnut and a little on the bucky side. His name is Red. He is so beautiful. We can work with him and make him a good horse. We sure had fun watching the rodeo today. What a bummer school will start very soon. Our calves are getting bigger. Dad has to work up in the cities. Dad said it wouldn't be much longer. Than we will be full time, dairy farmers. There is a chance we can buy some bigger cows. He can quit his job, and be at home all the time.

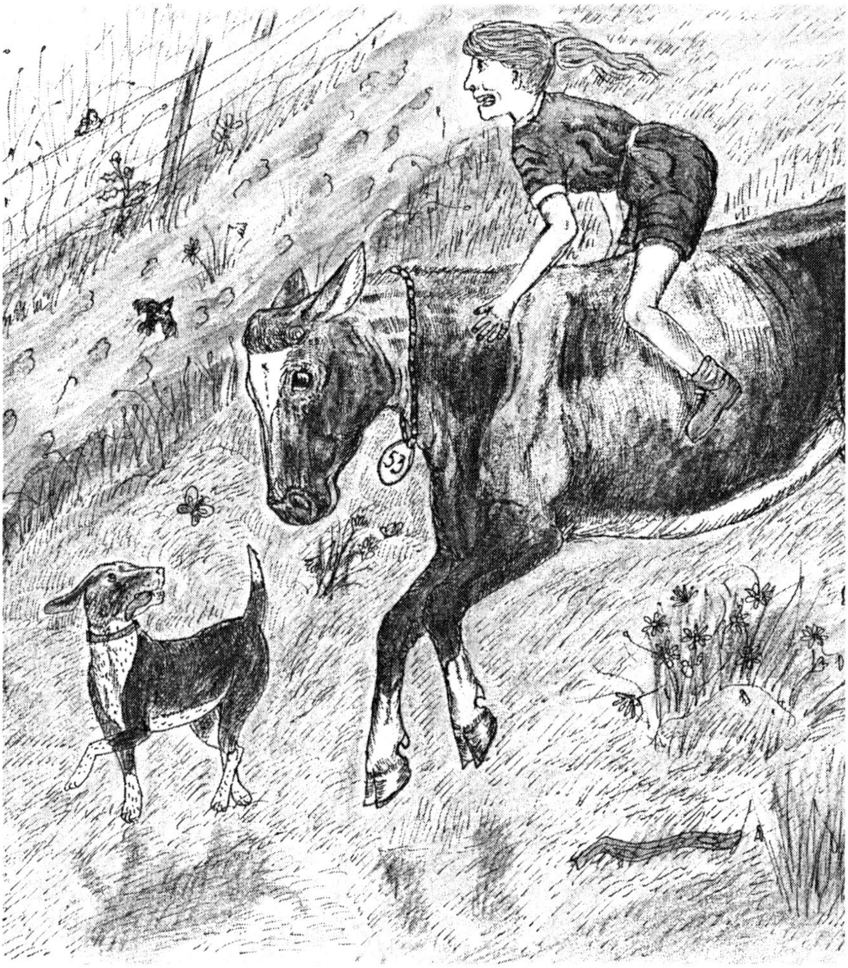

Chapter 6

▼

Reading, Writing, and Friends

"Betty, you went to Tennessee. Really?" I raised my voice to talk over the school bus loudness of many voices. I smiled; I'm thinking how neat Betty is. My first best friend, since we got our farm. Just think we met on the school bus. We have almost been friends for two whole months. We're in third grade together. "Yeah, we go there every year. Pop's talking about moving back to Tennessee someday," Betty smiled and moved her thick, long, brown hair to the side. "I'm glad you're my best friend," said Betty. I shook my head yes and smiled from ear to ear.

"Gee-whiz, this bus is noisy!" Charmon sat by us holding her ears.

"Hey, Benny. Could you slow the bus down a little and watch those bumps!" I hollered loud enough. Benny looked up in the rearview mirror and smiled, shaking his head.

"I'm sorry. I just can't do that. Because I'll fall behind schedule," Benny smiled then looked at the road as he shifted the bus, accidentally grinding the gears. We all looked at each other and giggled, holding our mouths. Betty noticed something different about me. She started starring at my right eye and pointed.

"What happened to your eye? It's a yellowish red color? I didn't go to school for a week because Dad and Mom were afraid someone would call them in for child abuse," I pulled my hair over to show Betty.

"Wow, that's a shiner. How did that happen?" Betty asked as she gently moved my hair with her hand.

"Well, while you were down in Tennessee. For two weeks a lot of neat things happened," I smiled.

"But what happened to your eye?" Betty looked at me with her light blue eyes.

"It happened about two weeks ago. When you were down in Tennessee" I raised my voice over the noise to be heard. "We were playing Indian and deer. We were the deer and Nyla was the great Indian hunter," I gestured throwing a spear into the sky.

"Well, then what happened with your eye? How did she do that to you?" asked Betty.

"She took her homemade bow and arrow and a spear and shot it at us. If she hit us, we were dead," I smiled and shrugged my shoulders.

"Nyla missed me. I was too fast. We were having fun." Charmon laughed.

"Well, I was running and jumping like deer. Nyla threw her spear in the sky and hit me in the eye," I felt so embarrassed. I smiled and touched my eye lightly.

"Boy, I bet that hurt," Betty smiled

"I saw stars. It felt like my eye got poked out," I lightly touched my eye. "Ouch". "Is it still that noticeable?" "It still feels a little sore yet,"

"It's a little noticeable yet, Patches!" Charmon smiled and teased.

"Patches? Where you'd get that nickname from?" Betty couldn't help laughing.

"Well, last week we went over to the neighbors, the Roth's. They live in that big old school house on corner. Anyway, we went over to their house to visit and his sons were visiting. They rode their scooter down in the basement. I ran into the wall a few times when they let me ride it. One is Bob and the other one is Ron. Bob is the cutest and funniest, and they were clowns together," I giggled. "They teased me and called me Patches because of my eye," I laughed and felt embarrassed.

"Well, Patches seemed suitable for now," Betty laughs. The gears on the bus started to grind and we were coming closer to the school.

"Look Betty, I brought my overnight bag!" I raised a large brown paper bag and showed it to Betty.

"Oh, so neat I can't wait, I've got a lot more thing's to tell you later," I smiled.

"Look I brought my jacks," She said and pulled out the jacks and a small ball out of her pocket. Soon the bus was making more turns and more stops. Then the bus started to left turn in the school driveway. The bus slowed and stopped while everyone piled in a tight line to get out.

"Hey, can you hurry up and sign this so I can get out of gym today!" Betty handed me a note so I could sign it before we got into the school. I took the note and signed it on my book.

"I'll sign it Alvin Garlan, right," I carefully forged Betty's Dad's signature and smiled.

We got off the bus and went into the school. We walked through hallway. Hung up our jackets on some hooks and put our stuff up on a rack. So we could go into the classroom.

"I hope Mrs. Hawksford isn't crabby today like she was last time I was in school," I sighed.

"Yeah, she gives me the shivers. She is like Dr. Jekyll and Mrs. Hyde," Betty shrugged and shook her shoulders as she smiled. We were walking in the hallways getting to our classes.

"Hi Ann. Hi Michele and Hi Penny. See you guys in class," I waved and they waved back as we walked into the classroom and sat down in our desks. The 3rd graders sat by the windows in two rows. The third grade was so big they were put with the fourth grade class. We had separate homework from the fourth grade. We had to wear dresses: pants were not allowed unless you were a boy.

She stood about five-feet tall with gray curly hair. Floral patterned dresses adorned her slightly plump body and with her glasses, she looked dignified. Mrs. Hawksford was usually in good humor, but when wasn't she was like Dr. Jekyll and Mrs. Hyde. We made a good effort to stay out of her way that day.

"Today is Friday October 12, 1968," announced Mrs. Hawksford gracefully while taking her pointer. "We all knows what that means, don't we class?" She smiled at the class.

"We have a spelling and math test today?" Penny raised her hand.

"That's right. It's also library day today. Hope you brought all your library books?" Mrs. Hawksford added. We already had our math test, and then the first recess bell rang. We went out to recess and played jacks on the cold cement with our bare knees.

"Are you ready for the other tests today Betty? I'm nervous." I threw the ball down and hurried to pickup the jacks.

"As ready as I will ever be." She took her turn by tossing the small ball and picking up five jacks. The recess bell rang, "Rah-ling." All the children ran and scrambled back into the classrooms. We sat in our desks and did our spelling test. Mrs. Hawksford announced the words slowly and we were to write them down. I felt rushed, nervous and could remember some of the words. I erased and rewrote some of the words. I tore the page erasing trying to correct my errors. "Oop's!" I whispered. It was hard because I was hungry. The smell of the lunchroom was overwhelming and made it hard to concentrate. The bell rang again and we were free to eat lunch and go play outside.

"I'll meet you girls in the lunchroom I've got to get my bag lunch in my overnight bag." I grabbed it and noticed it was a little squished and compact like an oblong ball. Ann, Penny, Michele, Betty, and I all got our lunches and sat down at the same table. We sat and talked about everything, and how we thought we did on the tests. I especially was excited about going over to Betty's house.

"Hey, Judy. Aren't you going to eat lunch?" They all looked at me wondering what was in the lunch bag I felt like I was under the spotlight.

"What's in the mystery bag?" Ann leaned over smiling with her blonde curly hair and glasses.

"Well, to tell you the truth, I'm afraid to look at it myself," I took it from under my right arm and slowly put the squished bag on the empty space in front of me on the table.

"Oh, your lunch looks so good today. Green beans, macaroni and cheese, hotdog and bun," I closed my eyes and took and big whiff. "You guys are so lucky, to have hot lunches," I said unhappily.

"Come on. Let us see what's in the mystery bag?" Betty smiled.

"Betty, what do you have in your lunch bag?" I asked.

"I've a got peanut butter and jelly sandwich, chips, and cookies," Betty smiled, licking her lips. She slowly emptied her bag on the lunch table.

"What do you have in your lunch, Judy?" Michele raised her eyebrows and smiled. I then slowly unwrinkled my squished brown paper bag. They started to eat their lunches, still curious as to what was in my bag. I reached in the bag slowly and pulled out something large that resembled a sandwich or whatever. They all looked down at it wondering what that was.

"Oh, it's a sandwich!" Ann burst out laughing.

"It looked like you were pulling out something you were afraid of," Betty started laughing.

"Well, let's see what kind of sandwich it is?" Ann was so curious. I slowly opened the wax paper wrap; that held the thickly sliced, white homemade bread. It had white chunks of something embedded in the bread.

"You know, I think this is suppose to be potato bread," I picked out some of the potato chunks.

"What's that smell?" Ann wrinkled her nose.

"And it's cut about an inch thick!" Betty laughed. I laughed at the way they were making fun of my lunch. I then slowly opened it and hurried to close it back up, they all looked and totally gasped. I felt on the spot and a little embarrassed.

"Oh, you don't want to know," I gulped.

"Come on. What's in the inside of your sandwich?" Ann begged. I then opened the one-inch thick cover; they all stared and put their spoons down. Their eyes were peeled on the sandwich and their mouths wide open.

"You've got to be kidding!" Betty was totally awed.

"Nope, this has happened to me before," I smirked, feeling embarrassed.

"What is that?" Penny asked as she pointed her finger down at the sandwich. They all looked at the sandwich, in total awe. It's gray-brown, thickly sliced, and it had taste buds all over it.

"Oh yek, I think it's my Mom's famous cow tongue sandwich!" I wrinkled my nose. I took the sandwich and put it back into the wax paper and put it back into the brown paper bag. "I think I'll just eat my apple. I'm not hungry anymore," I slowly removed my apple out of the bag. I wiped the sandwich residue off the apple. I was mortified; I quickly tucked my bag under my arm. I looked up at the ceiling, and quietly whistled. I started jiggling my foot, with impatience waiting for the others to finish.

"Let's hurry. We only have 15 minutes of recess left." Ann said and we all hurried out the door to finish the recess. That day went fast "Thank God for Fridays," I thought to myself.

"Boy, that was quite a day. I'm so glad it's done," I sat down in the seat next to Betty and Charmon as the bus started to move.

"I am so glad it's done. I just couldn't deal with it any longer," Betty opened up the bus window, and took a big breath of fresh air.

"Judy, I wish I could have stayed overnight too," Charmon sighed.

"I know, but Dad said one at a time and next time would be your turn," I shrugged my shoulders and I didn't care. The bus made a few stops and finally it stopped in front of Betty's driveway.

"Finally we're here. Charmon, I'll see ya tomorrow," I waved to Charmon and the other sisters sitting in the back.

"Remember. We're picking you up early tomorrow because we're going to an auction." Charmon waved and looked out the window as we got off the bus.

"So why are you guys going to an auction, tomorrow?" Betty said as she walked backward facing toward me.

"I guess were going to get some cows more or something," I smiled as if Betty's question was silly.

"What kind of cows are you going to get?" Betty asked curiously.

"We're going to get some dairy cows, so we can start milking," I proudly smiled.

"Well, let's go to the house and change our clothes, and after supper, we'll go take a walk!" Betty said excitedly.

We walked into the house, which was small like ours, but had a more modern kitchen. The sweet sugary smell of cookies greeted us as we walked in. They were oatmeal cookies with raisins. Her mother was preparing a meal of meatloaf, mashed potatoes, and peas.

"Betty, remember to do your studies and come down for dinner." She had a southern Tennessee accent. She was about 5 foot 10 inches tall: It was easy to see where Betty had gotten her height. Her long white hair hung down, covering her back.

"Mom, don't you remember we're having Judy spend the night?" Questioned Betty.

"Well, I reckon I've forgotten. Well, nice to meet ya Judy. I've heard so much about you," Her mom stood there stirring the cake mix for the dessert. I looked around and saw that the house was in order. Pictures of Jesus were on the wall and a large Bible sat on a coffee table in the living room. Betty stood in the doorway between the kitchen and the living room and talked to her mom.

"Where's Pop?" She bumped the doorway, asking her mom questions.

"He'll be back. He went to town!" Her mom started the mixer.

"Oh, that's right. Sharen is spending the night with another friend of hers" Betty added. As she grabbed 2 cookies. " Thank-you, mom. We're going for a walk."

"Thanks Mom, Judy and I are going to take a walk!" Betty grabbed two cookies.

"Hey, here's Pop." A car pulled up and a chunky, dark, curly-haired man with dark eyes got out of a white car. He held a large bag of groceries in one arm and a bag of potatoes in the other. A little brown and white spotted dog jumped up and down to welcome us.

"This is my sister's dog." Betty bent over and petted the dog.

"Hi Pop, I'd like you to meet Judy Ford, the one I told you about," Betty said as her dad handed her the potatoes.

"Well I'll be. It's about time we've got to meet you. You're all Betty's been talking about lately," He said. She walked fast hurrying up to put the potatoes into the kitchen on the countertop.

"I'll see yah later, Pop. We're going to take a walk." Betty hurried out with two more cookies. We took along walk on the long country road. And talked about what we were going to do, the next few days. On the way back we smelled the supper and hurried our pace. We came in the door, and washed our hands. The table was neatly set. We all sat down in our places. Betty's dad was at the head of the table. We all prayed, and enjoyed the meal. I sat there shy and smiled, enjoying the family's jokes and conversation.

"That was a good meal. Thank-you." I said as I got up from the table with Betty.

"Your welcome, Judy. I'm glad you enjoyed the meal." Said Betty's mom.

"Your mom is a great cook and your dad is very funny." I said as I walked with Betty. We're going up stairs to play "Monopoly." Said Betty.

"Okay, write us once in a while, remember bed time is 9:00." Laughed Betty's dad. We played some games and looked at the clock. "I can't believe that you go to bed so early on a Friday night," I said as I grabbed the brown paper bag, and put on my pajamas. We went to bed even though it was only 9:00.

"What did you think of Mrs. Hawksford today?" Betty said as she turned off the lights.

"I don't know but I think she was, a little cranky. Get a load of those nylon socks she wears," I laughed. "Yeah, they're rolled up above her knee, how do you suppose she keeps them up"? Betty giggled.

"I don't know suppose the fat on her legs holds them up," I replied and Betty let out a laugh.

"And her glasses, She always has a chain to hold them on her neck," commented Betty.

"Do you think she hangs them on her because she might sit on them!" Said Betty and I laughed.

"This bed of your sisters is very comfortable." I lay in the soft bed.

"Why, thank you," Betty added as she pulled the covers higher. "So where's this auction going to be at tomorrow?" Betty asks, lowering her voice.

"I don't know. Somewhere by Prairie Farm I think," I cleared my throat.

"How many cows are you going to get?" Betty yawned loudly.

"I think enough to fill our little barn. Maybe about ten of them," I added.

"Judy, what's this about you guys getting a pony?" Betty raised her voice.

"Yeah, he's a red chestnut and a show pony," I lay there smiling.

"Have you ridden him yet?" asked Betty as she stretched.

"Well, he's a little bucking bronco. All my uncles tried to ride him and they all got bucked off". I pulled the covers over and then laughed quietly. "I suppose someday I'll ride him, he's a halter show pony,"

"Did you ever hear about the story of Ed Geene?" Betty said pulling up the covers.

"I don't know who this guy was. What did he do?" I whispered.

"I heard something about him. My Mom heard about him on the radio, a while back. "He killed some women, thinking they were deer," she scratched her head.

"What do you mean?" I shivered a little, rubbing my arms.

"He went around killing these women skinned them and hung them up in the basement." Becky said, sounding grossed out.

"Yeak, you mean he ate the deer meat. Or lets say he was a cannibal." "Awg. " I swallowed and shook. "Yeah, he fried it up and ate it. Then he had a shop where he sold lamp shades of human skin!"

"Yek, totally gruesome! Where did this guy live?" I gulped.

"I think somewhere near Milwaukee," Betty shook a little.

"Well, I'm really glad we moved from down there and came up here," I giggled.

"You know I'm glad you did to or I wouldn't have met you," added Betty. We looked at the clock and discovered it was late.

"Hey, it's almost one o'clock a.m. maybe we better get some sleep," Betty pulled her covers up to her head.

"Yeah, that's a little scary. Maybe we better get some sleep if I can," I turned on my side.

"What time are they coming to get you?" Betty asked.

"I think about nine-thirty a.m. I better tuck in." I stretched and yawned.

"Good night, Judy." Betty started to roll over.

"Good night Betty," I rolled over to get some sleep and excited about tomorrow. I looked around the bedroom and the moonlight lit through the curtains. The night-light looked like an orange. Betty was hitting some heavy zees and I couldn't keep my eyes open any longer. My eyes closed and I started hearing clanging, and banging about in the kitchen.

"Good morning, Judy," Betty nudged me to wake me up.

"Good morning, Betty. Smell that breakfast!" I took a big whiff. We hurried up and dressed because the smell of pancakes and bacon. Our stomachs started growling.

"How was your sleep last night?" Betty asked. "Good" I answered. "Good morning girls, how was your sleep I heard you giggling and talking all night," Her dad laughed, drank his coffee, and read the paper. I sat down and enjoyed the delicious breakfast.

"Thank you all for having me over. I enjoyed everything, Oh here's my ride, and I've got to go! Thanks again!" I exclaimed as I ran out to meet my family.

Chapter 7

▼

Going to an Auction

I tightly squeezed into the cab of the yellow stub nose Dodge pickup truck and we were off to an exciting new adventure. My first cow auction! Oh how neat. We're going to get a herd of cows and have a dairy farm like our Uncle Johnny.

"Well, did you have fun over at Betty's house?" Mom asked cheerfully.

"Yea, I had a good time. We talked all night and ate cookies and cake," I patted my belly and readjusted my seat on Mom's lap.

"No wonder you feel heavier," Mom laughed. The truck drove for a while. Mom navigated until we found some signs that directed us to the auction. We finally turned and went down about a mile and were drawn to the cars parked on each side of the road.

"Wow, there must be around fifty or more cars parked along the ditch," I pointed and I couldn't believe my eyes.

"Dad, are we going to buy some cows today?" Charmon asked.

"Yep, we're going to get us a herd of Guernsey cows because they're cheaper than Holstein cows and we'll save money." Dad smiled and started to park the pickup truck.

"This is so neat, we're at our first cow auction," Ann exclaimed.

We then piled out of the truck and followed Mom and Dad up to the auction. Dad stopped at a trailer, signed in, and got a number. The crowd was thick; some of them inspected the furniture on the lawn, the dressers and antiques.

"Gee, smell that sloppy Joe's and potato salad," I took a whiff, looking for the food.

"Do you think Ma would give us some money?" Charmon scratched her head, wondering.

"Mom, could we get some money so we could get something to eat?" I asked.

"Heres a couple of bucks for both of you. Enough to eat on," Mom reached into her purse and pulled out the money.

"Thank you, Mom we love you," I kissed her on the cheek as I fisted my two dollars.

"Just ask for more if your still hungry," Mom smiled and gave me a hug. "Just go to that trailer over there by the barn, and follow the smell." pointed Mom. I felt so excited, but hungry.

"Two sloppy Joe's and chips and a soda pop," I asked the lady at the concession trailer. I licked my lips.

"Charmon, what do you want to do now," I smiled as we ate our sloppy Joe's. Some dropped all over my blouse.

"Let's go and see what cows Dad's going to buy?" Charmon started to walk to the barn.

"Wait up, I've got to throw this napkin in the garbage." I threw it away and ran to catch up.

We walked into a hallway that had two doorways. On the left, the door to the milk house was closed. We slowly opened the milk house door saw that everything was so clean and in its place. The smell of fresh, warm milk filled the air. A milk chart hung on the wall it with a lot on numbers on it. Some were bigger numbers than others. Next to the chart was the big silver bulk tank. We peeked inside of it, noticing it was cleaned out nice and shiny.

"Wow, everything is so nice and neat. Look, he uses Surge milk buckets," I reached down and touched the nice clean assembled buckets.

"Let's go check out the cows. Let's see what Dad's going to buy," Charmon opened the milk-house door and closed it behind. We walked to the doorway that leads to the barn entrance.

"Oh, this is really nice. It's so white in here," We stepped down on the clean cement walkway. That led down between some cows stantioned up. We slowly stepped down. There were two cows stantioned on each side of the walkway. I petted the one on the left, as we walked through. She jumped a little in her stall.

"Wow, so many pretty brown and white cows." I said as I looked down the walkway. "Oh they are so clean and pretty, and they each have a number on their hips," I said as I observed.

"I wonder how many cows are here?" said Charmon as she started to count. "It looks like about thirty Guernsey's."

"Look Nyla and Dad are checking the cows out," I walked over to Nyla.

"How come you are squirting milk into your hand Dad?" I asked curiously.

"Well, I'm checking out the cow for mastitis, that is when bacteria gets inside of the udder. It causes curdling in each quarter and makes the cow sick " He milked each teat into his open palm. "That is why I'm checking out the cows." Dad answered.

"Look. Above each cow has a name and her milk history and when she is due to freshen," said Charmon as she pointed up at the little signs above each cow.

"About how many cows are we going to buy today?" I said as I held the cows' tail for Dad, so she wouldn't hit him in the face.

"Well, I'm hoping we get about ten or eleven of them to fill our barn." He said as he got up out of the stall. And went over to the next cow, numbered seventeen.

"Nyla, mark number fifteen down," He said as he continued to check out number seventeen.

"She's got a good history. Her name is Daisy. Dad, I think we should get this one," Nyla suggested as Dad continued to test her.

"You know, I think she would be a good choice. Nyla, write this one down too." Dad checked the next one over number eighteen, and shook his head. "No, not this one, she has too low of a bag." replied dad.

"Dad, I think we need about five more choices. Maybe six just in case some else out bids you." Nyla wrote a star by the cows her and Dad thought were good choices. Good histories, breeding, and condition of udder. Uncle Johnny let him know what to look for, when going to an auction.

"Dad, how come you got that number in your pocket?" Charmon asked.

"Well, you have to sign up for the number and pay for the merchandise before you leave the auction." Dad went to the next stall and kneeled down.

"Charmon and I are going to see the rest of the place," I told Dad, even though he was busy trying to decide on another few cows.

"Judy, let's go and get back in time for the cows to be betted on," Charmon whispered.

"Isn't it neat? "We're going to get a herd of Guernsey's and we're going to milk cows tonight," I exclaimed as we ran out of the barn to check out the place and see what everyone else was up to. The yard had some household furniture, antiques, and boxes of odds and ends. Ma was by the boxes on the ground checking through them. We went around the silo and there was a field full of farm machinery, tractors, manure spreaders, and wagons. Then we went to check out some of the buildings, wondering if there were souvenirs to take home.

"Look at that cool old truck Bud is looking into," Charmon pointed and we ran over to it.

"Bud, what are you doing?" I asked, leaning up against old blue truck.

"I'm checking out this Studebaker pickup truck. Dad said he was going to get it if it's cheap enough." Bud kicked the tires, checking them for the tread.

"Is Dad going to buy a tractor too?" I asked.

"Yeap, that little gray International tractor by the big red Massy Ferguson." Bud pointed.

"Neat! Charmon, we better get over to those cows. They're going to start auctioning off," I said as I nudged her arm. We ran to the barnyard in the back of the barn.

"We'll see ya Bud. Have fun," I turned and waved at Bud. We ran to the back of the barn where a huge crowd of people gathered, surrounding around a snow fence. A flatbed hay wagon was parked by the barn cleaner for the auctioneer to stand on.

"Wow, it looks like a lot of people are interested in this sale," Charmon said, nudging my arm.

"Let's sneak in by the snow fence and see which cows Dad's going to buy." I squeezed between a big man and a tall man in farm bibs. Charmon squeezed on the other side of me.

"Hey, little girls, we were here first," the big man moaned as he looked down at us.

"Oh well, we won't be here long. We are just watching," Charmon answered back. We moved around until we found a comfortable spot to watch in between the snow fence. The auctioneer got on a small wagon and a couple of guys with wooden canes got in the little snow fence pen. The first cow had hurried out the door and some people stood in front of the doorway so the cow wouldn't go back in. The auctioneer started the bidding at two hundred dollars and ended the bid at four hundred dollars. Dad showed his number and the auctioneer bobbed his head and pointed his wooden cane at him.

"S-o-l-d, to number 143!" the auctioneer yelled. Dad smiled and they handed him a small piece of paper, with the cow's number on it.

"We now have our first cow and we've got ten more to go," Dad gloated. Soon another cow and another were brought out until all of the cows were sold. Dad had purchased about eleven head; he was pleased by the smile on his face. They ended with the calves, followed by the machinery and the other remaining things. Dad followed the auctioneer and bid on other things for the farm. It was now six o'clock and people started to leave. Dad already arranged a trucker to haul our cows to their new home. We all squeezed back into our little Dodge and wondered about the other stuff Dad bought. Dad hurried home with the pickup and we all got out in a hurry.

At about 8:00 o'clock, a big enclosed cattle truck pulled in the driveway. Everything was all set up and ready for the first milking. The truck backed up to the barn and a ramp pulled out of the bottom of a door. The cows were all mooing and kicking around inside, causing the walls to shake.

"Okay, let them out one at a time so we can find a stall for them," Dad hollered to the truckers. They shook their heads yes in agreement to what he said.

"I want you kids to stay out of the way until the cows are in their stalls!" Said Dad, as the cows were unloaded. When all the cows were in the barn, the ramp was pulled up. The trucker talked to Dad briefly then drove off. The cows were now in their new stalls eating the feed that Dad had put in the front of them. He stood there in the open doorway with his hands on his hips and smiled. "We're now in business"; Dad rubbed his hands together.

"Ann, get the new milk buckets and Ma, get the milk house ready and bring in the milk cans," Dad called and gestured to everyone. "Someone get the milk strainer. Let's hurry, these cows need milking." "Someone get a small ice cream bucket and put soapy water in it and get a wash cloth."

"I will, Dad!" Charmon ran up to the house, all excited to see what our new cows would do. Dad plugged in the vacuum pump. To create suction to run the Surge milk buckets with. It made a loud put-ting noise. Dad took the first Surge milk bucket and plugged it in to the valve overhead and turned the valve on. Soon the milker started to make a cha-cha sound. The bucket resembled a silver spider with four legs in the front of it. It was the shiny silver color made of stainless steel. Nyla took the other one and followed his instruction. She then put an adjustable belt on the cow to hang the bucket on it. The milk machine had four suction cups that were put on the cows' teats. The milk machine swayed a little and it made a loud sucking sound. Nyla massaged one of the quarters of the cows' udder to encourage milk flow in the cow. When the quarter felt empty, she removed the suction cup.

Soon all the quarters on the cow were finished and Nyla disconnected the black rubber suction hose from the overhead valve. She carried the big silver milk machine across the shallow gutter.

"Well, let's see what number fifteen will give us," Nyla said as she slowly balanced the large milk machine on her knee. Raised one of the suction cups and expelling a loud air sound, she balanced the lid and slowly poured the rich warm sweet milk into the bucket. Bubbles came to the top.

"Wow, she's a good producer. Nyla had to pour some of that into another bucket," I exclaimed in disbelief, rubbing my eyes.

"Ann and Ellen, I want you two be in charge of the milk cans and the milk house." Dad filled the other bucket with some milk still in his bucket.

"Now make sure there is a milk strainer filter in the milk strainer so we don't get the inside of the milk cans contaminated," Dad directed them as they each grabbed a pail of milk.

"Boy, these are some heavy milk pails. It feels like I'm going to pull my arm out of socket," moaned Ann.

"Well Ann, if you think that is so hard, you should balance this heavy bucket on your knee," replied Nyla.

"Now girls, there is no time for arguing. Let's bring the cans to the barn. Then carry the can to the milk house when it's full," Dad explained as he put the milker on another cow and carried another empty milk can into the barn. Ann closed the lid of the full can and carried it into the milk house to the cement water cooler.

"Gosh, It's a good thing they have two handles on these old milk cans," Ann urged.

"Well, they still weigh a ton when they're full," Nyla exclaimed.

"Boy, even the milk can feels warm after it's filled with warm milk," Ma laughed.

"Dad, are we going to turn these cows out tonight being it's so late?" Nyla asked.

"Well I think we should. They can get some of that green grass tonight," Dad added.

"What time do we have to get up tomorrow morning?" Nyla asked.

"How about six o'clock a.m.," Dad sighed, and wiped his brow.

Dad and Nyla carried the last milk can to the milk house and Ann found her new little black and white kitten. She named" Kay Kay" she was given from the neighbor, Alvin. She put some fresh milk into an old pie tin and showed her new kitten where the milk was. Her delicate little tongue lightly licked the milk and Blacky came along and finished it. The cows were all let out and the barnyard light was turned on to see where direction the eleven-cow herd was headed.

"I hope we have enough milk cans for tomorrow morning," Dad shrugged his shoulders.

"We filled about six and a half milk cans. We have five left for tomorrow," Nyla replied.

"I'll call the creamery first thing in the morning and order more." Dad thought aloud. That night we were very tired. We washed up ate a quick supper, of hotdogs and went bed as soon as we got in the door. That night I was just too tired to write anything in my diary. Maybe tomorrow.

"Girls, it's time to get up. Charmon and Judy, go out and bring the cows up to the barn for milking," Dad said cheerfully at 6:00 the next morning.

"Coming Dad, already? We're still tired from yesterday," Charmon moaned and stretched.

"Charmon, shucks, I'm not putting shoes on. I'm running barefooted," I yawned. We got up out of bed and hurried down stairs. Then we went out to the pasture looking for the cows'. The air was cool, and thick with moisture. As we walked through it, it felt like a fine mist, dampened our face. Our feet got wet and cold our toes were turning pink.

"Gosh this grass is wet and cold. Look, I think I see something, over there. Oh, there they are. On the hill," I pointed them out to Charmon.

"We're in luck. It's foggy and damp out and the grass is cold and dewy." "But, Charmon, these cow paths are dusty and dry. Try to stay on them," I added.

"Let's see, I see six of them here and seven of them over there," Charmon counted. "Come on, Bossy, Time to get up." Charmon kicked one with her barefoot, "ouch!"

"I got a stick. Some of these cows don't want to get up." I tapped one of the cows' hips.

"Oh step in the spot they were laying. Its so warm." said Charmon as she warmed her cold feet on the spot where one of the cows were laying.

"Charmon, watch out it's a thistle patch around here. Ouch!" I picked one out of my toe.

"Well, finally they got the idea." Said as Charmon put her hands on her hips.

"Look! Red's got a stick in his mouth and is helping us chase these cows in," I giggled.

"Gosh, I guess he isn't such a dumb pony after all," Charmon laughed.

"Good. The barn door is open. Hey, that's a warm cow pie," I exclaimed and it squished between my toes. I followed the last cow in.

"Here Bossy. Come bossy," Dad called out loud. The last cow finally walked into the barn. Charmon and I waited outside until they were all in their stanchions. Nyla swung the door open and the cows were their stanchions. Nyla scraped the fresh green droppings into the shallow gutter. It was clean enough to start milking the cows. Dad put grain in front of the stalls to make it easier to put the cows in their stanchions.

That morning, milking had gotten done early. A big refrigerator truck pulled up that said "Stella Cheese Co." Clayton, Wisconsin on it. That was a milk can truck for Grade "B" milk. Dad explained to us earlier the difference. Grade "A" the milk you see in the stores is from milk stored in bulk tanks. The farms are very clean and up to the states high standards. Grade "B" milk is in milk cans. This milk is from farms where neatness isn't the high point. This milk is often used in cheese and other dairy products. It was very hard to farm with milk cans. I know that Dad would find an easier way to milk these cows.

That day we could see a routine develop. And see a lot of frustration of having enough milk cans.

"There's always a better way. We won't do this forever." Exclaimed Dad.

Dear Diary   October 14, 1968

I can say this, entry in a few words. Farming is not easy. It's hard and rewarding. What the heck I Love it. Even though we may complain. We have freedom and room to run wild. Our new cows look so pretty, out in our pasture. Dads said were getting more cows later. If were lucky we'll find a farm to rent close by.

Chapter 8

The Blossom Farm- Early Summer of 1969

Sweat dripped down my freckled nose like beads of raindrops. My hair separated on my forehead, drenched with dampness from the humidity of the day. My tank top stuck to my back like a wet washcloth. I stared for the moment, dwelling on the fact that milking cows tonight will take longer than usual. We started chores late, and the back of my legs stuck to back of my thighs. Hum…a mosquito danced around my ear, annoying me I swiped at it.

"Ouch, dang flies," I slapped my leg as hard as I could. That slap stung more than that fly bite. Then clunk! "Owh!" The cow I was washing hit me in the face with her tail and she was about to do it again.

"Betsey, I'll teach you. I've had enough of this!" So I grabbed her tail, took a twine string that was in my pocket, and I tied it to her leg. "Smack!" The cow behind me hit me in the back of the head.

The Blossom Farm- Early Summer of 1969

"Ouch! Is there no end to this suffering?" I was so tired that it felt so good to kneel. It was just too much work to get up. My bare feet under me were getting numb, stiff, and pink.

"Hey, Judy! What are you going to do? Fall asleep?" Nyla laughed. "Where are your shoes anyway?" Nyla smiled and shook her head. Nyla always wore a farmer's hat she was the oldest. Always seemed serious in nature at times, a medium build bold features. Nyla was very much like a sergeant in the army. The neighbors always claimed they could hear her bellow echo in the woods several miles away. She was milking the big Guernsey cow across the walkway directly from me.

Chaa-chaa-cha was the melody of the Surge milking machine. "Moo-moo" Betsy bellowed, demanding more feed. Her stomach expanded like a balloon while I was leaning my head against her and I almost fell over.

"Whoa, I guess I better get up," I yawned.

"Well, get up and get the lead out!" Nyla demanded. "Hurry up and let those finished cows out. It's like a sauna in here!" Nyla took off her hat and wiped the sweat from her forehead.

"I can't help it. I'm so exhausted, Nyla," I whined.

Nyla got up with a full milking machine and poured it into to a big silver bucket. The fresh warm milk smelled like it was warmed on the stove. Then Ann would take the bucket and bring it into the milk house and pour the white gold into a big silver strainer, which was perched upon a large 300-gallon bulk tank. I then reached up and grabbed Betsy's protruding hip and pulled myself up slowly.

Splash! Cold water hit my red-hot face, sending a cool awakening shock through out my body. I stood there with my mouth wide open, totally surprised.

"Charmon!" Why I'm going to get you!"

"Oh no you're not!" She hollered and ran out the milk house door to refill her empty plastic bucket. I jumped out of the stall as fast as I could and threw my washcloth on the barn floor and took my Kemps ice-cream bucket of soiled water. I was soon right behind her in the chase. She was then in the milk house refilling her small plastic bucket. Before she could finish filling her bucket, I took my bucket and swung it as far back as I could and I swung it forward. The water was released into the air like a waterfall and covered Charmon from head to toe. The gray water turned her white shirt gray. So I turned and ran as fast as my tired legs could carry me. I ran out the barnyard door to fill my bucket in the stock tank. Then splash! I felt my back saturated with cold water before I could pursue.

"Hey, Judy you better get in here and wash some more cows," Nyla demanded. When I stepped back into the barn, a wall of water quickly hit my face.

"Hey that's not fair!" I yelled, seeing Ann run up to the milk house.

"Ha-ha-ha!" Nyla laughed out loud.

Charmon snuck on another side of a cow Nyla was milking. The milker started to make a loud suction sound; Nyla hurried to remove the suction cup. The minute she stood up Charmon took her bucket of cold water and splash!

"Why you little rat!" She laughed and took off her drenched hat. "I'm going to get you!" Nyla hurried and removed the milker and jumped out of the stall. She set the milker on the walk and ran after Charmon and grabbed her bucket. Charmon ran and hid and Nyla took the bucket and filled it with cold water.

"Splash!" Ann looked totally surprised because she was now saturated. Ann was very fine boned and taller than the rest of us, with strawberry blonde hair. Ann had the narrowest piano fingers. Mom had claimed she pulled them to make them delicate as they were. Mom claimed she was the prettiest. But today it didn't matter: we were all saturated like four wet rats. We stood in front of barn and we felt cool for the first time that day. We laughed so hard we almost rolled on the grass on the hard ground.

"It's so hot. Do you believe we put up 600 bales of hay today? That's what I figured on the counter," Ann shook her head and put her hands on her hips.

"Where's Dad anyway?" I asked.

"Oh, he's cutting down more hay on the forty acre farm," sighed Ann.

"Where did you think he was, at home making us homemade ice-cream?" laughed Nyla.

"Do you think he will forget us again over here tonight?" I asked. "Gosh, since he rented this farm. He gets so busy elsewhere. He runs late and sometimes forgets us."

"Oh well, if he does it's only a 10 minute walk from here to home, no biggie" Charmon added.

"We're more than half way done with milking these hot cows. Let's talk torture," Nyla added wiping her brow and waving at a fly. We stood outside of the barn a little while, listening to the radio echo and the cows bellowing.

"Temperatures were up in the high 90's today with 80 % humidity. Tomorrow will be clear to partly cloudy. This is Ron Erickson with "WCCO Radio 8-3-0" St. Paul, Minneapolis."

"Georgia, Georgia, sweet Georgia on my mind with this old sweet song with Georgia on my mind" The radio echoed.

"Charmon and I need to stay outside for a while or we're going to faint," I took a deep breath and gasped.

"Okay, take your time. We're almost done," Nyla answered. Nyla and Ann hurried back to the barn to finish the chores and get done as soon as they could.

"Wow, look at the stars. Aren't they really neat? Look there's the Big Dipper." I pointed to the sky. "Charmon, just think God made all this. It looks like a million lights." I said.

"They're very beautiful. Feel that breeze," Charmon closed her eyes to feel the breeze.

"It sure feels good. Smell that sweet aroma of that fresh cut alfalfa hay. Smells good enough to eat," I closed my eyes and took a whiff of fresh air.

"Judy, only if you're a cow," Charmon nudged my arm and laughed. A moment later, she gasped, "The lights went on. Hey, did you see that? Look at the old green farm house on the hill."

"Gosh, the door just opened and slammed and someone is coming down the hill," I gulped. "Charmon, did you know if someone was still living here?" I grabbed her arm.

"No, Sometimes I heard noises but I wasn't sure if someone really lived up there." Charmon gulped.

"Well, there must be someone up there because whoever it is, is slowly walking down the hill right now," I rubbed my eyes.

"Look how slow that person is walking. It looks like an old man, Judy," Charmon pointed.

"Charmon, he walk's a little like Tim Conway on the Carol Burnet show," I laughed.

A little old man slowly approached us. He looked rough with unshaven whiskers and must have only stood about five foot tall, with a rigid appearance. He finally stood in front of us and we could see he wore thick wire rimmed glasses. His blue overalls were worn and tattered and he wore an old blue farmer's hat.

The Blossom Farm- Early Summer of 1969 69

"Charmon, do you believe this? I really thought the house was empty." I whispered and nudged her arm a little. We stood close to each other. We both wandered what this old man was going to tell us.

"You girls better get out of here. There's a real bad storm coming in real soon," the old man warned in a hoarse voice, as he cleared his throat.

"But the weather man said the weather would be clear tonight," Charmon argued scratching her head.

"It's coming from the south and it isn't going to be very friendly. Strong winds, lightning. It's bad, I tell you, very bad!" He shook his finger to the sky.

"What's your name?" I asked the old man.

"Ole Olson! May, I suggest you girls head home right now!" He demanded and sternly shook his finger at us. We both got excited and started to run to the barn to warn Nyla and Ann. We stopped and turned to thank Ole.

"Look, Charmon. He's gone and the light's off in the house on the hill," I gulped and Charmon grabbed my arm.

"That was really creepy," Charmon gasped. We started to feel a wind pickup, see lightening and hear rumbling of thunder in the far distance. We were feeling very anxious and ran into the barn.

"Nyla, is it okay with you and Ann if we just go now. We'll run home. We don't need a ride!" Charmon begged and looked very frantic.

"Yeah, I'm not waiting for Dad either!" I added nervously.

"Well I guess, Charmon you can go. Judy I need your help." Nyla said as she shook her head. "Judy, don't look so disappointed. We still have work around here to do."

"Why do you want to go now? Why can't you wait for Dad?" Ann stood there with her hands on her hips.

"We were outside cooling down and this old man came out of that house on the hill," Charmon explained nervously.

"Charmon, don't forget to tell her his name. Ole Olson!" I added.

"What's the deal? Are you guys serious?" Nyla demanded.

"He told us we better hurry home because there's a big storm coming!" Charmon exclaimed.

"Bull, there is no storm coming tonight. The weather man said so," Nyla shook her head. She was kneeled down by one of the last cows. "But I suppose I could let a couple of you go."

"Ann and Charmon you two can go. We'll wait for Dad to pick us up, and I'm not walking home!" Nyla rolled her eyes. "Ooh, I guess I got a few goose pimples." Said as Ann rubbed her arms and started to pace a little.

"Ann when you were hauling milk to the milk house, did you see those guys talking to an old man outside?" Nyla rubbed her chin.

"No, but it seemed like they were talking to someone. Nyla, Charmon left and I'm going right behind her. Judy you will have to spray things down in the milkhouse. The wind picked up a little and I'm going too! Bye!" Ann turned and ran out of the barn.

"Charmon looked real frantic. Ann got scared. Judy was there really an old man outside from that house on the hill?" asked Nyla as she got done milking the last cow. The cow started to move back and forth in the stall. Nyla unstanchioned the anxious cow and the cow turned around. She jumped over the shallow gutter. She raced out the door and bellowed to the others.

"Yes, there was believe me, it's true! I exclaimed and told her more about the incident. Nyla just looked at me scratching her head.

"I don't know if I really believe you." Said Nyla as she dumped the last milking machine. I brought that last pail of milk into the milk house. I sprayed down the milkhouse. The lights started to flicker and the wind picked up, blowing inside of the barn. The thunder and lightening were overhead. Nyla hurried to finish scrapping the barn down.

"Well were finally done. Do you think Dad forget us again? You know he gets busy." I started to rub my goose pimples on my arms.

"I know Dad rented this farm cause it's close to home, but I didn't think anybody still lived here, did you?" Nyla shook her head and rubbed her goose pimples.

"No. Look, it's starting to rain in blankets. Oh bummer, the lights went out," I grabbed Nyla's arm and she pushed me away.

"Judy, get a grip." Dads, is still coming to get us. We stood by the barn entrance watching the lightening.

"Good, truck lights! He remembered us," I smiled. We ran to the Studebaker as the storm started to pickup even more. They opened the truck door and the rain poured in.

"Hurry up and close the door!" exclaimed Dad.

"Are we glad to see you Dad. We really thought you forgot us!" Nyla signed a breathe of relief.

"I'm, so sorry girls. I was very busy getting the last of the hay cut down," explained Dad.

"Charmon and Ann told me something about this old man warning them about a storm coming in.," " I thought I better get over here!" Dad started to shift the gears of the old Studebaker.

"Dad, do you know an Ole Olson?" Nyla asked him, wiping her wet face.

"No not personally, but I heard he used to own this farm about 30 years ago." Dad started to drive slowly.

"Whoa, that's a mind blower is he still alive?" Nyla sat back into the seat.

"No Nyla. His son was telling me there was a tornado that killed him right after he had got done with chores one night," He stopped the truck a little and pointed to a big oak tree. "What I understand is he just stepped out to check the storm and it just sucked him up and twisted poor Ole around that oak tree that is still standing this day," Dad explained.

"Why would you ask?" Dad took off his hat to scratch his head.

"You two look a little spooked," said Dad as he started to speed up to leave the driveway.

"Its nothing, Dad. You really don't want to know. Its just one of those nights," Nyla shook her head, her eyes huge as saucers.

Dear Diary   June, 28, 1969

It's been a hard long day. It was very hot and miserable. Oh, Lord I do believe in ghosts.

I hope we never run into Ole Olson again. My hands are sore and red for helping with the haying.

Well I'm tired I've got to go to bed. That thunder is loud and the wind is very scary. I pray that everything will be standing tomorrow.

Chapter 9

Our Second Autumn- Of 1969

"Charmon, look at that cloud! It looks like a whale." I pointed at the sky, lying on my back.

"Judy, that one looks like a bird," Charmon pointed to the far cloud in the East.

"Snort." A big cow smelled my feet and turned away to go the other way. "Shew, get out of here, cow." I kicked at her with my leg.

"Gee, Judy, she must have smelled your stinky feet," Charmon started laughing.

"Charmon, how long do we have to watch these cows?" I sat up to look at the cows to see that they don't cross our boundary.

"I think Dad said all day until milking time," Charmon yawned.

"Well, how do we get something to eat?" I asked, as my stomach growled. "Errh."

"Mom's going to bring us some sandwiches and something to drink at lunch time," Charmon got up to chase a cow that was crossing our boundary between us.

"Boy, this is so boring. Dad said he use to watch cows when he was younger." I added.

"Yeah, it looks like we're an invisible fence. Dad said since were low of pasture. We should watch the cows. So they have more grass to eat. " Charmon exclaimed. " It makes me think about stuff that happened. Like last year. Seeing that tractor tread on the ground. It reminded me of what happened to Nyla. Said Charmon as she took a deep breathe.

"I think we walked three miles from the store so we were late for chores that day." Exclaimed Charmon.

"That sure scared me when Nyla fell under the big tractor wheel and her butt went up in the air," I shrugged, and rubbed my arms.

"And you ran home on the gravel road barefooted to get some help," Charmon remembered.

"It was only about a half mile and didn't the tractor just keep going until it hit a telephone post?" I took a deep breath.

"She had tractor tread all over her face. I'm glad that she was okay." Said Charmon as she chewed on some grass.

"Yeah, Nyla sure has a hard head. A cop checked her out and brought her to the hospital." I remembered.

"I'm so glad that's over with. Do you remember Red?" Charmon questioned.

"Who could forget him! He was one of a kind," I scratched my arm and smiled.

"Yes, that was really sad. Last year deer hunting. Lenny Mello shot Red. Charmon shrugged. "He was starting to turn out to be a good pony. I sure miss him. He was so pretty."

"Yeah, just because Dad wouldn't let Ann date him," I looked down at the ground. "I wish we still had him." I felt a loss and sadness.

"Dad put a large ad in the paper that said, 'Wanted the person who shot the kids' pony." Charmon recalled.

"The reward was, what, fifty dollars, wasn't it?" I said as I got up and ran after a cow that crossed our boundary.

"But we got lucky to get that gray and white mare from the Roth's," Charmon said as she stretched.

"Yeah, she bucks every-time you want to ride her. But you just get back on and go for a good pony trot," I giggled a little.

"I don't like that about her. She's frisky for an old mare," Charmon smiled.

"I figured out a way to stop her from bucking right after you get on her." I pulled the grass.

"How did you do that?" Charmon scratched her head.

"I made a small corral out of big sticks from that lazy oak tree. I put her in it and there is no space for her to buck," I smirked.

"Neat. Then does she buck after she's out of the corral?" Charmon asked curiously.

"No, she just gives a good trot. That's all she knows what to do," I said.

"Hey, I think I hear the Studebaker coming." Charmon jumped up and wiped the dust off her shorts. Charmon turned and looked toward the driveway and the Studebaker turned in it.

"I'm so glad we still have Sissy." I jumped up and shook the dust off my pants.

"Just think Dad almost got rid of her too. Blacky had all those puppies. Blacky didn't have Sissy until later," Charmon smiled.

"It's a good thing too because Sissy is a lot prettier than the other black puppy Sassy," I shrugged.

"Look. Mom's bringing us sandwiches." I pointed to Mom as she walked toward us with a brown paper bag and a jug of water.

"Mom, I'm so hungry I could eat a horse and so bored I can't stand it," I yawned.

"Thank you, Mom for the sandwiches. We're so hungry." Charmon took a fast bite and drank some water.

"I'll be glad to let you girls know that you won't have to watch cows tomorrow," Mom smiled.

"Boy, that's relief. What are we going to do tomorrow?" I took another bite of my bologna sandwich and smiled.

"We're going to have a threshing party. Everyone is going to come over and help with putting up our oats." Ma took the brown paper bag and water jug.

"If you two want more water, just go up to the Blossom house and there's an outside facet." Mom pointed to the green house across the field.

"Okay, Mom, thank you for everything. We'll see ya about supper time," I waved.

"Gosh, I'm not going up to that house. No way!" Charmon swallowed.

"No, I don't think they can pay me enough," I rubbed my arm.

"Gee, do you think Ole Olson was really there or did we imagine him being there?" Charmon scratched her head.

"I don't know and I don't want to know if that was really Ole Olson," I shivered. "What's threshing anyway?" I swatted at a sweat bee.

"I don't know but I hope it's a lot more fun than this job and walking cows back and forth from farm to farm," Charmon said as she swatted at a fly.

That afternoon, we finally finished watching cows out on the Blossom hay field. We then herded the cows into the barnyard through the open gate and than put them into the barn. That evening when the milking was done, we'd herd them over to the forty-acre farm. The cattle could graze on the field that was fenced in with electric fence. The Blossom farm was an extra eighty acres and only a quarter of a mile from our forty-acre farm. Dad rented it when he expanded his herd from eleven to thirty cows. Tomorrow we were to find out what threshing was.

The next day, a large giant metal gray machine was pulled into our two-acre oat field by a green John Deere tractor, driven by Alvin Hurtle. The machine was very tall and very long; with four metal wheels painted orange. It had a thick pipe protruding out of the top of it.

Charmon and I walked around the two-acre oat field that was behind the house. We went to greet Alvin as he parked his big threshing machine. The John Deere B roared and echoed as he backed it to where he wanted it to be. We stood and watched the big gray machine as it found its right position on the field. Bud was on the tractor with Alvin and helping in pull the pin out of the hitch.

"Wow, that's quite a machine," I hollered, looking up and shading my eyes against the machine.

"Yeap, she's really old too!" Alvin looked down from the big tractor as he turned it off in order to talk to us.

"What are you going to do with that thing?" Charmon asked with her eyes shaded over from the sun.

"Well, today I'm going to bring my binder over and we're going to cut the oats in bundles." Alvin sneezed, took his kerchief out of his pocket, and wiped his nose. "And then you girls get to shock the oats so it will dry out," Alvin took off his hat and scratched his head.

"What's shocking?" I asked, scratching my sweaty nose.

"You'll find out. I'll be back with the binder," Alvin nodded, started up the tractor, and drove out of the field onto the road. Bud got off the tractor, ran through the oats up to his armpits, and then up to the house.

"Hey, Bud! You're not supposed to run through those oats!" Charmon yelled.

"Dad said you'd flatten out those oats and make it hard to cut them down," I added.

"So! I don't care! I'm hungry right now." Bud answered as he continued to hop through the tall yellow ripe oats.

"Taa-taa-tah," echoed the John Deere B between the two farms. Alvin was on the tractor, pulling a machine behind it. The tractor then turned into the field and slowly crawled through the field. The awkward machine slowly bounced behind the tractor. Alvin parked the tractor and the other machine behind it. Dad walked out and invited Alvin into the house for some lunch and coffee.

"Well, it's all ready to go. It's just a matter of getting out there to get started," Alvin shook Dad's hand and they started talking about other things and laughing and walking up to the house.

"Girls, time for lunch. Hurry we got a busy afternoon ahead." Dad turned and waved.

"I wonder how this thing works?" I touched the metal round bar. The front of machine was flat and had a blade in the front. A roll of twine string on the side went around to where the grain would be cut rolled into bundles, and dropped onto the ground.

"Nyla said this thing is also called a Swather," Charmon added.

Lunch was enjoyable especially since Alvin was over. He was always a nice person with a good sense of humor. Dad and Alvin always hit it off and often worked together doing fieldwork, one helping the other.

"Did you want to hear a dirty joke?" Alvin joked, and then realized that there were children everywhere.

"Well, maybe you better not," Dad hesitated.

"Two pigs fell in the mud!" Alvin started laughing then swallowed his coffee. We all started laughing and finished eating. We were all ready for our big afternoon.

"Oh, Grandma and Grandpa, Uncle Danny, and Aunt Hazel are going to come over. To help with the oats." Mom added as she started to clean up the plates.

"About what time?" Dad asked.

"Oh, about two o'clock," Mom scraped the dishes.

"By that time we may be done with the field work. I was hoping they would come earlier," Dad shook his head and started to head out the door. "Now kids, I want you to come out and we will show what to do." Dad headed out with Alvin and all of us, except Mom, followed one after the other, slamming the screen door behind. We all followed Dad and Alvin out to our plush yellow ripe oat two-acre oat field. Alvin and Dad talked and decided they need a tractor with a wider front end. Alvin ran over to get the Massey Ferguson, which only took five minutes. They moved John Deere over by the threshing machine so it would be hooked up by the flywheel. The flywheel is positioned on side of the tractor. It is circular in shape and the edge is flat. It is a power source for running machinery. By hooking a belt up to it.

The red Massey Ferguson was hooked up to the binder and Alvin started to drive the tractor through the oat field. He went very slowly and pulled a handle that protruded from the machine. The Swather, or binder, started to rattle and rumble as the blades started to slide back and forth. We stood there, observing the machine as it started to cut and roll the grain into small bundles and dropping them to the ground very slowly. The bundles were now called shocks. As the binder slowly dropped bundles, Dad and Nyla started to pick up four of them at a time. They stacked them up against each other like a tee-pee with four shocks. Dad hollered so we could hear him over the loud tractor. So we started picking up the bundles and stacked them according to Dad's instruction.

"Isn't this fun, Charmon?" I laughed as we held the rough light bundles.

"Wow, there are a lot of bundles out here." Charmon looked around with her hands on her hips. We kept shocking until the field was covered with a lot of little tee-pees. The sun set reflected an orange tint on the light, yellow oat stacks. It was time to get the cows in the barn. It was a short day, different from all the others. Grandma and Grandpa drove in about suppertime. Milking went quickly with a little help from Uncle Danny and Aunt Hazel. They promised they would be back the next day to help finish the threshing and bale up the straw.

As always, we milked the cows that next morning. Again at noon, we headed out to the field this time we were to harvest the bundles and bale the straw. Alvin connected the big thresher with the John Deere B's flywheel with this big, huge, long belt. He started the John Deere and the belt rotated and flopped about. Alvin then pulled a lever and the big threshing machine started to rumble.

"Now I want you kids to load those bundles on the wagon so we can feed them into the thresher," Dad instructed. Nyla took our John Deere B and a flat hay wagon and drove around the field where we were to load the bundles. The bundles were then cut and fed into the thresher, which rumbled and rattled. It spit out dust and straw and empty hulls and kept the oats inside of its large, tin belly. When that was full Alvin took his flat bed wagon with sides on it; the thresher spilled the dusty yellow oats onto the wagon. As it poured the oats onto the wagon, Dad moved the oats around and the dust flew everywhere like a smoke screen. Grasshoppers jumped everywhere and green weed seeds dropped in the pile. Dad got on the tractor and pulled the load up to the barn by the silo where he had built a small bunk inside of the silo room.

Uncle Danny helped shovel the oats into the bin by the door from the wagon. The oats piled nicely in Dad's new wooden oat bin. We ran our hands through it and it spilled through our small hands, tickling between our fingers. The green seed clung between our fingers and a grasshopper sat on my palm by my thumb. It moved around deciding which direction to hop off. As it jumped, I felt the push off of its small little back legs. It left a little brown spit mark on my dusty palm.

We continued our routine until all of the oat bundles were put through the thresher and the straw was baled and put into one of the sheds. We all were covered with dust from head to toe.

That night came fast. Dad took us through the bumpy field with the old Studebaker.

"Ha-ha-Hee-hee!" I laughed so hard, bouncing around in the back.

"Ha-ha! This is fun!" Charmon laughed so hard she almost rolled of the back.

"Hee-hee!" Bud giggled.

"Oh bummer, we're going toward the Blossom farm again," Ann stopped laughing. The truck stopped in front of the barn and we all got out. Dad drove off while we waved.

"Awe shucks, all the cows aren't up." Nyla shook her head and hit the dust off her cap.

"Judy, Charmon, please go out there and get those cows. We'll put these into the barn." Ann pleaded.

"Okay, Judy you go that way and I'll go this way," Charmon asked.

"Look at Sissy, that crazy dog is running around with a stick in her mouth chasing cows," I laughed.

We went everywhere searching for those cows: we looked high and low. I got through the woods and there was a steep hill. The wind blew and the smell of the stinkweed that grew as tall as me beside the woods, the smell was overwhelming. It smelled as if something died. "P.U.!" I walked up the hill and a found some delicate little flowers with a thick green stem.

"Oh lord, these little flowers are a beautiful orange," I kneeled down to smell them. I touched the soft little flower and it responded to my light touch and closed its blossom on my index finger.

"Whoa, it grabbed my finger," I touched another and it did the same with a soft and firm grip. It opened up again when I removed my finger. After a while, I realized was getting dim. I got up, remembering why I was out here.

"Come Bossy," Charmon's voice echoed in the woods.

"Come Bossy," I called, my voice echoing. I heard some branches breaking in the very far corner of the pasture. Then I heard some mooing and movement and saw the last three cows.

"I found some cows!" I hollered and it echoed in the woods.

"Come Bossy!" I called and they followed me back to the barn, like they were lost in this big pasture. What a big day this turned out to be.

Dear Diary   August 28, 1969

These last two days were hard and fun. Hard work isn't always boring. Just think what we did in harvesting the oats. Our Grandpa probably did when he farmed. Its real neat to think that farming is quite the family thing. It really brings the family together. We're one big team. Thank you God, again. I'm tired and time to turn in.

Our Second Autumn- Of 1969

Chapter 10

Grandma and Grandpa's House

I woke up to nature's call. I rubbed my eyes as I fumbled my way down the steps. I had come into the kitchen and saw Grandma stoking the old wood stove, where a huge pot of coffee sat on the stove. Grandma was lifting the lids of the stove "clunk" as she was throwing paper and small chunks of wood into it. I tried to quietly walk behind her to go out to the outhouse.

"Ouch," I stubbed my big toe on Grandpa's big black Red Wing boots. "Oh, I didn't see ya. Judy, are you getting up or going back to bed?" said Grandma as she put more wood into the old wood stove.

"It sure is cold this morning. You better grab a sweater to go out to the outhouse," Grandma added. "Finally the fire started. I better get a bucket of water from that water pump so we can have some drinking and wash water," Grandma took a metal bucket and opened the screen door and I walked out with her. I felt the cold, brisk air on my legs and up my back so I ran as fast as I could. Grandma stopped by the water pump and started to pump the gray metal handle.

As the roosters were crowing, I hopped around the chickens as I ran to the little gray narrow building and touched the cold wooden door. I took my choice between the 2 separate holes with the cold seats. I could hear "Brock Brock" outside of the outhouse as I finished my business.

I hurried to run back to the nice warm house, tripping over chickens which were everywhere in my path. Poochy, Uncle Danny's dog, raced me to the door and I let him in as I entered and jumped over the boots blocking the door entrance.

"The coffee's on. I'm going to gather the eggs. It's a lot of work with five hundred chicken's," uttered Grandma.

"I'm going back to bed, Grandma," I yawned and rubbed my eyes and smelled the coffee as I headed back up the steep steps. I went back to sleep only to wake up to the sound of eggs frying on the stove and bacon splattering. Charmon followed me down the steps, only to find we were the only two that hadn't had breakfast.

"Good morning, Charmey and Judy. Say, you're just in time for breakfast," Grandma busily scraped out the scrambled eggs out of the cast iron frying pan.

"Now, when you girls go out to play, don't go by the ponds or the chicken house. I don't want anyone falling in the water. Or disturbing the chickens laying eggs." Grandma put some bacon and toast on our plates.

"Judy, I'll race you outside!" Charmon finished her breakfast first and ran out. "Wow, there sure are a lot of chickens out here. Yek! You got to watch where you step." The chickens were everywhere Aunt Kitty and Aunt Hazel would throw corn to the chickens. Uncle Danny would butcher a couple for supper tonight and Grandma would clean them. A rooster started to peck at my bare knees so Charmon and I started to run back toward the house.

"Help, this rooster is trying to get us, Grandma!" Charmon and I ran as fast as we could to escape the big white rooster. He was tall and the feathers were ruffled on his neck. Grandma took a broom and went after that rooster as we escaped to the house for safety. Grandma had chickens for a couple of years. I must add it was messy. But we would run into the house and hear.

"Check for wood ticks!" Grandma would always say. Always after we were outside we would have to check for wood ticks. The farm had swamps, ponds tall grass, little trees and about one hundred million wood ticks. I would just step outside and run in the grass. We'd have to pull off about five or six of them. Charmon and I nick named Grandma and Grandpas farm. (Grandma and Grandpa 's wood tick farm.}

Uncle Danny's dog, Poochy was a medium sized, black and white speckled longhaired mongrel. He was the smelliest, filthiest, and fat wood tick infested creature. That dog seemed always old and grumpy. One time when Bud was younger he went by Poochy's dish. Poochy bite him Ma and Grandma took him to the hospital for stitches on his face.

Grandma and Grandpa's house was always the family reunion place. When people would start to leave, Grandma would warm some buckets of water on the wood stove and bring it out to the washtub. We were too big to sit in it so we would stand up and let Grandma wash us down. We were so glad when Grandma would put the towels on us, because it was so embarrassing.

Grandma was a little over five feet tall, was a medium built and salt and pepper curly hair, which was accented by her dark plastic rimmed glasses. A soft, raspy voice escaped from her always smiling, buck toothed mouth. Grandpa was also medium build with thin gray hair. Some things about Grandpa were constant: He always wore a cap, bib overalls and wire rimmed glasses. He also always chewed his snuff, and at times he bragged about his Red Wing boots. Grandpa did watch repair for a hobby. He worked for the railroad for 25 years. He loved old tractors, hunting and fishing.

They had a big white house, a gray barn, a wooden silo, a few rickety out buildings and a old gray outhouse. The driveway was about a half of a mile long and near the house, circled around a large Maple tree. Deer Park was a quaint little town just a few miles away. Some times we'd go to the park where they had white tailed deer in a large tall pen in the park. They were the reason they called Deer Park, Deer Park. People were free to feed them corn or treats. And that made this little town special.

"I'll see ya at Christmas," Grandma said as she gave us a big sloppy whisker kiss. And before you would know it. It was Christmas time again. We would always go there at Christmas Eve, and stay overnight.

"Ouch Grandma," as I would wipe off Grandmas kiss.

"Oh, I just love you kids." Grandma gave us each a hug.

"Well, Merry Christmas every one. Tomorrow night, we're going to the Christmas Eve program at the Lutheran church," Grandma pulled some cookies out of the oven.

"We're glad you guys could make in time. It's the Chovan tradition," Aunt Kitty smiled as she was standing in Grandmas kitchen. She was an attractive, woman with a thin build. Her plastic dark frames gave her a studious look, which contrasted her chatty nature but fit her well-organized life.

"Hey, Ann, Charmey and Judy come here. I've got to tell you something upstairs," Aunt Hazel waved. Aunt Hazel was unique and she always had a way with words. Mom's younger sister was the same age as Nyla. She was a chubby teenager with thin blonde straight hair, and wore dark plastic rimmed glasses. She always had scary stories to tell. She was active and involved in many things, such as reading palms, collecting antiques and going to auctions. We all ran upstairs and followed Aunt Hazel to her room. She instructed us to "Close the door!" We closed the door than sat down on the hard wood floor and crossed our legs.

"Any ways other night when I was asleep I was woke up by a light touch on my foot," said Aunt Hazel

"Well, then what happened next?" Ann crossed her legs and leaned forward.

"The circle of light, danced around room a little. I just laid there in my bed and watched this uninvited visitor. It got near the open window and flew out." Hazel took a deep breath. Hazel grabbed the stuffed bear and hugged it.

"I think it was some kind of spirit. Honest, it's true, I'm not lying," said Aunt Hazel. She wiped the tears from her red face. We sat and listened to Aunt Hazel. "Hum I smell some cookies." Aunt Hazel took a big whiff.

"Yum, Christmas cookies." Said Ann as she took a big sniff. We started to get up to open the door and go downstairs.

"Girl's! Come down and get some cookies," Grandma called as she put dishes away. The house was very warm and smelt of burnt wood and fresh baked Christmas cookies. We walked into the living room and saw Grandpa and Uncle Danny sitting on the couch. The Christmas tree was in the far corner. It had a few colorful presents underneath and the lights were so pretty.

"Hey, Judy. Stay away from those presents. Santa Claus is going to bring yours tonight," Uncle Danny, with his plastic rimmed glasses, and nice hair he joked around a lot.

"Everybody get washed up and ready, so we can go to that Christmas pageant right after dinner."

Grandma would say. The table was beautifully set, white tablecloth and Grandmas best china. It had a point-setta setting in the middle of the table. Everything was so warm and tasty. It was the best oyster stew I've ever eaten.

"Let's eat our oyster stew and crackers and let's get ready to go to the Christmas Eve program at the church," Grandma and Aunt Kathy started to prepare the meal.

"Lord, let's bless and be blessed. Thank you for this food. Amen." Said Grandma we all filled our bowls with the traditional oyster stew, and after eating, we went to the Christmas Eve program that night at St. Johns Lutheran Church in Deer Park. Younger members of the church played in the program. It was Grandma's favorite Christmas Eve thing to do. We all enjoyed the entertainment. When it was finished we walked out the door, they handed us a bag with peanuts, Angel food, and Christmas candy.

We arrived Grandmas and Grandpas house, and Grandma instructed us. "Kids, it's time to ready to go to bed. Santa Claus is coming tonight.

I went to bed wandering if I was going to get that stick horse and cowgirl outfit. We woke up early that next morning; the tree was plump full of presents. Dad and Mom brought ours with so we could open them with everyone else. Grandma already had breakfast on the table.

"Here, this one's for you kids," Aunt Hazel handed a big preset over to us.

"Oh, it's a toboggan." I pretended to act surprised.

"Kids, eat your breakfast dress warm, before you go out to play!" Grandma suggested. Bud and I hurried to go outside so we could go play in the deep snow. We started to slide down the hills. There was a big hill that was by a big frozen pond. Bud was the first to take the toboggan down the hill onto the ice. He slid down the hill very fast and he flew onto the ice. Then I tried it: I flew onto the hard ice. I laughed so hard because I couldn't believe how much fun it was. Then we both got on it and we hung on tight and hit the ice, causing it to crack a little.

"Oh, oh! I think it's time for some Christmas cookies," I laughed and Bud followed me into the house. We opened the door and the warm air hit our faces. We pulled off our winter coats in a hurry.

"Hey, Judy. You didn't open your present from Grandma!" Aunt Kitty handed me my gift. I had intentionally forgot. I knew what it was. It was flat, about ten inches long, and about three inches wide.

"Thank you, Aunt Kitty," I took it and slowly opened it. I tried to force a smile but I knew it was the same as last year: a pair of purple pantyhose.

"Uncle Danny, Charmon and I went out to the pond this morning and saw Santa Claus's sled and deer tracks on the ice," I was so excited to find proof. Uncle Danny smiled and giggled.

"It's true, Uncle Danny!" said Charmon as he stood there with her hands on her hips. Uncle Danny looked straight at her and smiled from ear to ear.

"Christmas dinner, everyone!" Grandma announced and we all sat up to the table. While the Viking's game played on television. It was turkey again, it was usually dry, but adding gravy moistened it. There were mashed potatoes, and a bunch of salads, with pies for dessert.

"This is the Chovan tradition. Let's keep the tradition," Aunt Kitty would always announce year after year. We were always gathered together. We were not perfect but we were family. We loved each other and spent many holidays together. We always felt God was there for us.

Bibliography

This book, tells a story about Judith Lynn (Ford) Sanson's life. She was born in 1958 in Milwaukee, Wisconsin. For many years, the family lived in town. Until 1968 they moved to a small farm. Farming became a new way of life. The illustrations are drawn from the author.

Moving from town to out in the country was the families dream. The move was 300 miles up to northern Wisconsin. Starting from scratch was an interesting struggle. The family started with a small farm and gradually worked up to a larger farm. Farming had its ups and downs. Strange and unusual things happened.

A car hit Judy. Did she survive? Nyla got ran over by a tractor, did she survive that? A stranger stopped by the farm one night. Or did he really stop by the farm? How does it feel to own your very first horse? How does feel to own dairy calves? What does owning a dairy farm entail? How does a child fit in on living on a dairy farm? Learn and remember how it is to be a child again. Feel the love and excitement of enjoying the life with farm animals. This book is truly fun to read. It is from the heart. The family will take you to different places. The illustrations were completed from the author. Photographs were added in the back. It's one book in a series of three. Enjoy!

Index

A second book of this three book series will be out in a short while look forward to it.

Those Rough Country Roads

What rough country roads lay ahead for the Ford family? What uncovered skeletons may lay hid in their family. What happened to the blossom that once thrived happily?

Growing up had its ups and downs, what become of the once content child. If you want to know and look foreword to the next up coming book. Please feel free to contact—(iuniverse.com.) And let them know what you want to read. Will this blossom wilt or will it grows with a little added fertilizer?

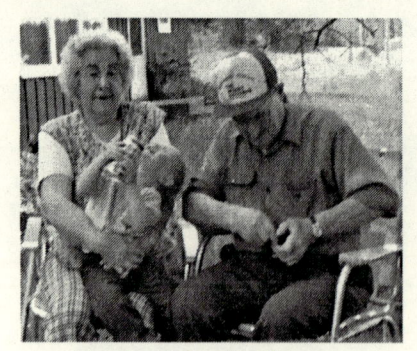

96   A Blossom from a Barnyard

Grandma & Grandpa Chovan

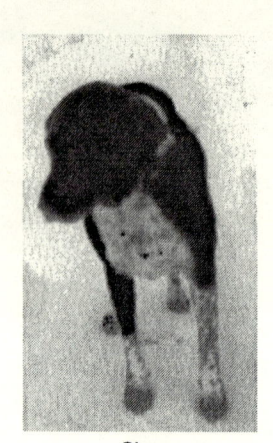

Sissy

Bessy

Uncle Henry, Jeanette and jersey heifer

Old wood stove

Index 97

Charmon on Red

Us girls with Brownie

1936 Massey Ferguson tractor

Our herd we raised.

Photos in 1968, Nyla, Ann, Judy & Charmon

9 780595 167609